CW00674191

Shift!

Powerful Stories of
Organizational Transformation

William James Press

LAS VEGAS, NEVADA

Copyright © 2016 by TMI International.

All rights reserved. No part of this publication may be reproduced, distributed, or transmitted in any form or by any means, including photocopying, recording, or other electronic or mechanical methods, without the prior written permission of the publisher, except in the case of brief quotations embodied in critical reviews and certain other noncommercial uses permitted by copyright law. For permission requests, write to the publisher, addressed "Attention: Permissions Coordinator," at the address below.

William James Press
8635 West Sahara Avenue
Las Vegas, NV 89117
www.williamjamespress.com

Quantity sales. Special discounts are available on quantity purchases by corporations, associations, and others. For details, contact the "Special Sales Department" at the address above.

Orders by US trade bookstores and wholesalers. Please contact BCH: (800) 431-1579 or visit www.bookch.com for details.

Printed in the United States of America

Cataloging-in-Publication Data

Shift! (Barlow)
        Shift! : powerful stories of organizational
transformation / edited by Janelle Barlow and George
        Aveling. -- First edition.
            pages cm
            LCCN 2015955722
            ISBN 9780971743229 (hardcover)

        1. Organizational change.   I. Barlow, Janelle,
        1943- editor. II. Aveling, George, editor. III. Title.
        HD58.8.S55 2015   658.4'06
        QBI15-600215

First Edition
20 19 18 17 16   10 9 8 7 6 5 4 3 2 1

All rights reserved. No part of this document may be reproduced or transmitted in any form, by any means (electronic, photocopying, recording, or otherwise) without the prior permission of the authors.

Contents

Foreword
Jim Kouzes, coauthor of The Leadership Challenge   vii
Foreword
Kostas Hatzigeorgiou, Global CEO, TMI International   ix
Introduction: Transformation, Change, and Culture
Janelle Barlow, President, TMI US   xi

Part I: Firing Up Passions   1

1. Transforming Internal Service with an Organizational Mission
   John Sabatino, CEO, TMI Australia   3
2. Reducing Churn by Transforming Complaint Handling
   Cynthia Nolan, Senior Account Director, TMI US   13
3. When People Are Passionate, Transformation Blooms
   Elena Khodko, Deputy Director, TMI Ukraine   21
4. Chinese Children, Dreams, and Teamwork
   Edmund Lai, Chairman, TMI China   31
5. Leading Quality from the Heart
   Conor O'Connell, Managing Director, TMI Ireland   37
6. Water Tanks and Passion
   Sally-Ann Huson, Global Value Proposition Manager,
   TMI International   43

Part II: Aligning Your Leadership Team   53

7. Leading Change from the Top
   George Aveling, CEO, TMI Malaysia   55
8. When Having Great Departments Is No Longer Enough
   Cynthia Nolan, Senior Account Director, TMI US   61
9. Of Service and Crêpes
   Alice Kaboth and Carolin Reiter, Consultants, and Bernward Mönch,
   CEO, TMI Germany   67
10. Aligning Customer Service across Multiple Borders
    Ariel Jasovich, Director, TMI Argentina   77
11. When Old Meets New
    Ayşegül Drahşan, General Manager, TMI Turkey   83

12. A Russian Bear Takes on Complaint Handling
    Jeffrey Mishlove, COO, TMI US   91

Part III: Shifting Mind-Sets to Transform Cultures   97

13. The Heartbeat of a Culture
    Edward Matti, Managing Partner, TMI Middle East   99
14. Racing toward a New Reality: From Sports Car to Formula One
    Racing Car
    Anna-Maria Pepin, Managing Director, TMI Switzerland   105
15. The Power of a Smile
    Janelle Barlow, President, TMI US   113
16. Exploring Is More Fun Than Attacking
    János Balázs Kiss, Managing Partner, TMI Hungary   121
17. It's Not Easy, but Cultures Can Learn to Soar Again
    Veronica Fernandez, Head of Consultancy, TMI Spain   129
18. From Good to Great
    Rossitsa Hristeva, Deputy Executive Director, TMI Bulgaria   139

Part IV: Making Transformation Stick   147

19. Let's Not Forget about Tomorrow
    Janelle Barlow, President, TMI US   149
20. Persistence Leads to Success and Sustainability
    Suman Sethi, Principal Consultant, and Sumati Malhotra,
    Marketing and Project Management, TMI India   157
21. Changing a Culture So Safety Rules Are Followed
    Victoria Holtz, CEO, TMI Latin America   165
22. Great Project Planning but Bad Coffee
    Mariska Hulsewe, Jacques Dumans, Consultants, and
    Wim Barendregt, Managing Director, TMI Netherlands   177

Part V: Transforming on a Personal Level   187

23. "The Little Match Girl" Gets a New Ending
    Johnny Hassinggaard Jensen, CEO, TMI Denmark   189
24. Investing to Bring Out the Winners on Your Staff
    Fransiska Atmadi, Managing Director, TMI Indonesia   193
25. Confessions of a Resistant Innovation Manager
    Danilo Simoni and Alessio Cavallara, Managing Partners, TMI Italy   197
26. A Goal Travels from One Part of the World to Another
    Janelle Barlow, President, TMI US   203

27. You Don't Always End Up Where You Thought You'd Be
   Azmi Omar, Head, Branded Customer Experience, TMI Malaysia   207

28. The Power of an Aha Moment
   Octavian Pantis, Managing Director, TMI Romania   211

29. My Turning Point—Transformation inside a Seminar!
   Meltem Şakarcan, CEO, TMI Turkey   215

30. You Just Never Know
   Janelle M. Barlow, President, TMI US   219

31. Learning to Be an Effective Leader Demands Personal
   Transformation
   Adriana Mendoza, General Manager, TMI Colombia   223

32. When Your Back Is Up against a Wall, It Can Be a Great Time for
   Transformation
   Tunde Rotimi, Head, Business Growth, TMI Nigeria   227

   Epilogue: From "Ugly Babies" to Transformation
   George Aveling, CEO, TMI Malaysia   231
   Notes   235
   About TMI   237

Foreword

Jim Kouzes, coauthor of *The Leadership Challenge*

My earliest memory of the power of stories was of my Danish grandmother—my mom's mom—telling my brother and me about how, unaccompanied, she crossed the Atlantic Ocean on a ship from Copenhagen to New York City when she was sixteen years old. She didn't speak any English, yet she managed to get from Ellis Island halfway across the United States to Audubon, Iowa. We never tired of hearing that story, which she often told us while making Danish pancakes—our favorite—in our kitchen in the suburbs of Washington, DC.

Grandma Loss was a force of nature. She was tenacious, tough, independent, and strong in body, mind, and spirit—which you have to be to grow up on a farm, cross a big ocean and traverse half a continent all alone, and live through two world wars, the Great Depression, the much-too-early death of her husband, and being a single woman who had to cook, clean, and do laundry for other people to feed herself and her two daughters. I learned a lot from Grandma Loss, but the lesson that transcends all others is how, despite what life throws at you, you can overcome adversity and make a better life for yourself and those you love. And, as Grandma Loss would never tire of reminding us, you also have to work hard to make that happen.

I thought about Grandma Loss when reading the stories in this book, how they are about a similar theme—overcoming adversity and making a better life for those you care about. The times are very different now, but the morals of the stories seem very much the same. Out of adversity can come transformation—a transformed life, a transformed organization, a transformed community, and even a transformed world—if, and it's a big if, you embrace it wholeheartedly.

Adversity introduces us to ourselves. Challenges and difficulties force us to examine our strengths and weaknesses, values and beliefs, and hopes and dreams. Sometimes we choose the challenges, like hopping on a ship to a new country, and sometimes they find us, like an economic depression, but when we come face to face with them and embrace them, we learn how powerful we really are. We learn that if we broaden the context, we can see that we're not the first to experience adversity. We learn that we can defy the verdict that we're doomed. We learn that if we want to transform something, we have to fully commit to it. We learn that we have to take charge of change and not let it take charge of us. We learn that it's a lot easier to handle when we engage with others and show that we care.

The stories in *Shift! Powerful Stories of Organizational Transformation* teach all of these lessons. They teach lessons of perspective, of mission, of passion, of dreams, of teams, of service, of heart, of persistence, of character, of diversity, and of so much more—including the power of a simple smile. This is a wonderful collection that celebrates the power of the TMI brand and the TMI global team—individuals and an organization uniquely equipped in the art and science of personal and organizational transformation.

Congratulations to all on the celebration of TMI's fortieth anniversary. The world is a much better place because of the work that you do. Just imagine what can happen in another forty years!

Foreword

Kostas Hatzigeorgiou, Global CEO, TMI International

Many business books have been written by commentators, thought leaders, and captains of industry about the knotty problem of successful change. But few books take the reader on a practical, "roll-up-your-sleeves" approach to transformation based on multiple case studies from around the world.

Written by consultants from TMI companies, this book takes the reader on a practitioner's view of transformation. We have been in fiercely competitive business arenas, facing challenges and working out how to make change happen. Above all, we have focused on how to make change sustainable. We have had to face the risk and fear of failure. And we have had successes.

Our consultants work in what is arguably the most complex space of all: the people and organizational transformation space. There is a saying: "It is a wise person who learns from experience. It is a wiser person who learns from the experience of others." We believe that this book has a definite place on the bookshelves of many readers who want to learn from TMI's experience:

- Leaders and leadership teams who face the daunting task of moving their organizations forward
- Mentors and coaches who want to draw on practical examples of transformation
- Change agents who need inspiration and ideas about how they can make an impact on people and organizational mind-set
- Transformation consultants who want to improve their craft

- Individuals who want to pursue and achieve personal transformation and wish to be active contributors to the success of their team and their organization

The most successful transformation initiatives demonstrate a coherent and consistent pattern. A fundamental and necessary requirement for the success of any transformation initiative is a strong commitment of top management toward the change process. This commitment flows through the organization's levels like a rolling stone, encompassing everyone. A sustainable cultural transformation demands that the change be pervasive. For cultural transformation to happen, all people in the organization have to be fully aligned to its shared values—vision, mission, beliefs, attitudes, goals, and strategy. They need to have a clear line of sight to the common objective of the transformation initiative.

Shift! shares the challenges, the practical steps, and the lessons learned during TMI's forty years of experience worldwide. This book contains examples written by thirty-five TMI transformation consultants from twenty-four countries around the world. These transformation stories span the areas of customer service, leadership, complaints, quality, and safety. The book shares stories of leadership and management transformation. It also shares stories of personal transformation that lead to happier, more fulfilling lives.

It is with humility that we share the distillation of our experience.

It is with excitement that we reveal the essence of our craft.

It is with pride that we present this book to the world!

Transformation, Change, and Culture

Janelle Barlow, President, TMI US

Organizational transformation is a little like a home remodel-ing project. If you have ever attempted to change something in your house, you know it is not a good idea to go at it halfway. Paint one room, and the whole house begs to be repainted. I sometimes say in jest that if you change one doorknob, you might as well give in and remodel your entire home.

The same is true of business change projects, particularly if they require changes in your organizational culture (how things are done). You will see this in the stories in this book. Many of these initiatives started with one relatively small change. Very soon, however, the change ricocheted throughout the whole organization.

If the proposed change does not engage the people in the organiza-tion, the change will ultimately fail. Statistics back this up. Approximately 70 percent of change efforts fail because people have not been engaged in the process.[1] In addition, if a change is not supported by the existing orga-nizational culture, culture will win—every time. And the organization and the people in it will revert very closely to the behaviors that were present before the change was implemented. Is it any wonder that many adopt the attitude of "Just wait. This, too, shall pass"?

> *Approximately 70 percent of change efforts fail because people have not been engaged in the process.*

So what is *transformation*? It is a term that is used in logic, design, mathematics, genetics, theatre, statistics, linguistics, politics, and business. In fact, if you use *transform* as a verb, it can be used in any field. In its simplest presentation, transformation is about change. In fact, these two words are used synonymously in this book.

The types of transformation we work with and write about in this book represent fundamental changes in how organizations conduct business through people. These transformations are closely bound to the culture of an organization.

Many organizational leaders believe they can drive transformation by simply making structural changes to their business operations. These structural changes could include massive reorganizations, mergers and acquisitions, or the establishment of detailed rules for how staff should interact with customers. For example, leaders who believe smiling by staff will achieve higher levels of customer satisfaction may say, "Let us all smile at the customers every time we see one." Yet those same leaders may rarely smile at the customers themselves. In their belief system, service rules are for customer-facing staff—not for themselves.

If customer-facing employees do not smile, however, perhaps the leaders are not taking into account that team members could be dissatisfied with how they are treated by their bosses. Perhaps these employees feel regularly abused by customers who are upset. After all, some customers scream at web pages that load too slowly or do not work. Some customers swear they

> Many organizational leaders believe they can drive transformation by simply making structural changes to their business operations.

will never do business with a company again if they are hit with fees that they feel are imposed far too frequently. The organization may have a long history of increasing profits at the customer's expense whenever it can. For example, advertising may draw customers in with promises that cannot be met by employees, though employees are expected to keep customers happy—or face getting reprimanded by their managers. Something has to give in situations like this. Smiles typically go first.

Sometimes managers do not support their people when they attempt to meet customers' needs, even though the managers state they want their staff to be empowered to handle customer complaints. The managerial structure often is based on a top-down command-and-control approach, which creates a reality where employees have to get permission to do just about anything for customers.

When a business needs to change, simply adjusting its structure or changing procedures will not guarantee a desired shift; culture must be considered in the mix. Figuring out how to align organizational cultures with behavioral transformative initiatives is TMI's expertise. When this alignment is done well, the newly restructured or redefined organization creates a synergy that yields sustainable and significant behavioral change. When we help people in an organization pay attention to their culture, we can help them translate their goals (words on a page) into staff performance (behaviors in action).

While our focus is not on organizational theory, at TMI we believe that when an organization embarks on a transformational journey, its culture must be understood first to see how it will interact with proposed structural changes and goals. If, for example, an organization's culture consists of a toxic relationship between staff and management, that toxicity must be addressed first. If the organization changes its policies and procedures but does not address how the culture must also change, the transformational goal is not likely to succeed.

As Peter Drucker once pointed out, "Culture eats strategy for breakfast."[2] In other words, culture will ultimately reestablish itself. Strategic changes that fly in the face of organizational culture will have difficulty succeeding in the long term. People are loyal to people and to the cultures in which they work. They are not loyal to policies and procedures.

Strategic changes that fly in the face of organizational culture will have difficulty succeeding in the long term.

When businesses seek out a transformation process, they do it mostly to have a different relationship with customers, to reduce costs, or to increase market share. As Peter Drucker said more than fifty years ago, the focus of a business has to be its customers. After all, he wrote, "The purpose of business is to create a customer."[3]

The stories in this book show how culture and structure can work together to create better relationships, to make things happen, and to swiftly transform an organization. At the same time, TMI consultants will be the first to admit that not all the ventures we undertake with clients are sustainable. Frequently we discover this only after we have been working with a client for some time. It is never pleasant to watch proposed transformation goals collide head-on with the reality of culture.

We know that transformation is never easy. Resistance to change grows strong and tall in most organizations. This is true even if the proposed transformation is needed just to keep pace with changes occurring in the external marketplace. Let us repeat a critical point: an organization's culture must first be analyzed to see how it will support or resist a proposed change. Only after incorporating this analysis should you move ahead with a proposed strategy.

We also know that transformation requires time. It does not happen in the blink of an eye. The process normally has starts and stops, as you will see in the examples presented in this book. Success comes when your people behave in ways that your competitors' staffs do not— because they do not have your culture. You can also think about your culture as your internal brand. In fact, Tony Hsieh, CEO of Zappos, says, "Your culture is your brand."[4] If you get it right, he believes, pretty much everything else will take care of itself. And Zappos is a company avid about its culture.

What Is TMI?

Founded in 1976 in Denmark, Time Manager International (TMI) is a classic "started in a garage" type of company—only in TMI's case, it was a basement. Claus Møller, his wife, Viveca, his brother, and some highly competent friends started the Time Manager company. It made the first planning tools to help people manage their time. The tools were great. Millions of people owned Time Managers, especially in Europe. In fact, they became so popular that *Time Manager* became a generic term for any type of planning tool.

But what really made the company successful were the two-day Time Manager seminars that accompanied the little black books. People organized their lives in these ring binders, carried the binders with them, and made huge changes both in their personal lives and at work. People attended the programs and then talked about TMI. Through word of mouth, the company grew exponentially. The programs were hilarious and instructive at the same time—people did not fall asleep in these seminars (and even after forty years, they still do not today).

The programs were funny and touching, and they showed people how to live in the modern world without destroying themselves and their families. People finished the programs and started taking responsibility for their lives. Our ideas and approach touched people in such a personal way that they transformed themselves.

Almost everyone involved in those early days of Time Manager International joined the company because of how he or she was personally transformed. I joined TMI in 1981 because I learned the lesson about taking responsibility for my life. That may sound so simple and mundane, but it meant that I took total control over the decisions I made, how I was with other people, and what I chose to do with my time and life. That is significant. We still hear examples like this in most of our programs, and you will read some of those individual transformation examples in this book.

TMI also had to transform itself because of changes in the marketplace. Very quickly, we were no longer the only company selling planning tools. So we moved into the customer service space. But even then, we did not just teach customer service techniques. Our Putting People First programs were about personal development—or, as we would say today, personal transformation.

One TMI client that has been written about in a number of books is British Airways. British Airways was a UK state-owned airline, ripe for transformation. Margaret Thatcher wanted to see changes in the bloated bureaucracy of BA, its bad customer service, and its even worse attitudes. Few staff members saw any need for the airline to turn a profit. An old joke that circulated at the time said that BA 747 planes were the best way to move four engines around the world, but they were not good for much else. Thatcher wanted the airline to transform itself and get ready for privatization and a public stock offering.

TMI had demonstrated its capacity for transformation the previous year with its work with Scandinavian Airlines. SAS transformed itself from a huge money loser to a multimillion-dollar profit maker by focusing on customer service aimed at business travelers. SAS is still going strong today. The SAS success helped TMI win the BA contract, and TMI was invited to deliver its two-day Putting People First seminar to more than thirty-eight thousand British Airways employees around the globe. Colin Marshall, then fifty years old, came out of the rental car market (Hertz and Avis) in the United States to lead BA. He was experienced at transforming companies in highly competitive environments. Marshall introduced several ideas to BA, including lounges in airports, business class, and a focus on fixing problems for the traveling public.

But it was Colin Marshall's focus on people, both staff and passengers, that was the key to BA's transformation. Regarding the Putting People First program he said, "I was anxious to inculcate its principles into the minds of front-line people—those who had direct contact with passengers, including people in customer-service jobs, check-in agents, flight attendants, pilots, and reservations agents."[5] Marshall was one of the first CEOs of a giant company who demonstrated a clear understanding that mind-set changes were crucial if customers were to be treated differently.

In fact, Marshall said at one point that BA needed to invest in a transformation project the size of TMI's Putting People First initiative every three years or so.[6] That was a significant conclusion to reach given the necessary resources that went into putting thousands of staff through a two-day program about attitudes.

Marshall was made a peer in the House of Lords in 1998 based on his success with British Airways. Sir Colin Marshall, Lord Marshall of Knightsbridge, passed away on July 5, 2012. Even though he was retired at the time, his passing represented a huge loss to the airline industry in terms of daring and innovation.

What Does TMI Do?

Typically, TMI works with organizational clients when strategic business changes need to be implemented in human behavior. Strategic changes can include changes to an organization's goals, mission, purpose, or strategy. Many times we are asked to work on customer service goals, leadership issues, or the updating of staff capabilities.

By no means do we attempt to implement all strategic goals. In Tom Peters's terms, we stick to our knitting. Our knitting involves branded culture, service, performance, and leadership—the human side of organizational transformation. Sometimes all of these get wrapped into one change process.

TMI has a sister company named TACK Global. TACK focuses primarily on sales, management development, and safety. Many of TMI's and TACK's licensees around the globe hold the licenses for both TACK and TMI in their respective markets. In these cases, we combine the expertise that is housed in each of these companies.

If you want help in assessing which big company to purchase next or which new IT system to purchase, we are not the people you want to see. But if you want to change your culture or brand your service, our experience in those areas covers much more than this book demonstrates.

Why This Book Now?

In 2016, TMI is celebrating its fortieth year in business. And we are celebrating in part with the publication of this book. Strip everything else away from us and we are a consulting and training company. We operate in about sixty countries around the globe, and we have been in business longer than most consulting companies have been able to manage.

It has been touch and go at various times for our individual country licensees, so we have used many of the same approaches on ourselves that we have applied to client work. As a result, the global operation continues to thrive. We thought it would be fun and interesting to share some of our memories of transformation work with our clients.

We asked our country managers for examples of transformation in their markets. Almost all responded, so this book includes a mix of stories from around the globe, some of which involve the biggest and most successful companies in the world.

Several of these stories are about individuals who came to training seminars we facilitated, from which they walked out transformed people. The story of a Romanian businessman who set a world record for distance triathlons is a stunning example of personal transformation, behavior change, and goal setting. (His name is mentioned, unlike in the other examples; he is a world-famous person, and you would be able to easily figure out who he is because of what he has done.) Other personal transformations are simple examples such as the story of a woman who saved her marriage after learning one simple technique that she applied in a significant way.

How the Transformation Stories Are Organized

Our stories have been divided into five parts:

Part I: Firing Up Passions. Our examples here include a top-rated Australian university, a metallurgy business, and a call center that is part of one of the world's largest telecom companies. We also look at a special event held in Shanghai in 2014 that fired up the passions of TMI and TACK consultants. One example involves a quality group within an organization that led from numbers but could transform only when quality came from the heart. Our final story in this part involves work we did years ago with Sun International on the border of South Africa. This transformation was remarkable because we had to bring together African workers who had lived most of their lives under apartheid and foreign managers who had incredibly low expectations regarding what service the workers could offer.

Part II: Aligning Your Leadership Team. Our first example in this part comes from a very successful bank that led a transformation process with its top team, our second example is about a top cruise line that is constantly looking for even higher customer service ratings than they already receive, and our third example is about a huge telecom company that saw the necessity for aligned leadership around service improvement. We also present an example that deals with leadership across several countries and a story about a Turkish company that needed to change its leadership style realities so it could attract and keep top young talent. Finally, we conclude with a story about a Russian bank that transformed its approach to complaint handling in a remarkably short time.

Part III: Shifting Mind-Sets to Transform Cultures. Examples in this part include the stories of a successful Middle East automotive group that wanted an even larger market share, a huge consumer goods company that had gotten complacent, and a magnificent cruise line introducing a new brand. We also present an account of a pharmaceutical company that transformed how it conceives of the original research it conducts. In the next story, our TMI Spanish team was invited back to work with a company that had a strong customer service structure but was in danger of losing it in the midst of the economic crisis. Our last example involves a Balkan States electric company that wanted to create a leadership culture that would enable it to achieve world-class performance.

Part IV: Making Transformation Stick. In this part, our examples include the story of a Native American casino that is the blue-ribbon-champion example of sustainability efforts. Next, we present the story about a midsized Indian bank in which TMI India learned, based on early rejection by the client, to sell in such a way that it ended up winning the client's business and influencing the company in the process. We also cover one of the most difficult transformation efforts—establishing a safety culture that is sustainable. We conclude this part with the story of a Dutch company that started off well enough but couldn't sustain its transformation.

Part V: Transforming on a Personal Level. The last part includes personal transformation stories. Some of them are heartwrenching; others may cause you to cheer. And some of these stories are about the individual transformations of people who work with us today at TMI. We are very happy their personal transformations led them to us.

We made a decision to not identify our clients, so any names you see have been pulled out of thin air, except in the cases of the Romanian triathlete, BA, SAS, and Sun International. We have not shared anything prohibited under the nondisclosure agreements we sign with all our clients. It is the narrative that is important, not the name of the organization.

Lessons Learned

We have learned a few lessons along the way, including those we've discovered by studying our own organizational transformation. This is not an exhaustive list by any means, but it provides a way to learn from transformational initiatives.

Lesson 1: Your Leadership Team Must Be Aligned

> *Every successful organization has to make the transition from a world defined primarily by repetition to one primarily defined by change. This is the biggest transformation in the structure of how humans work together since the Agricultural Revolution.*
> —Bill Drayton, social entrepreneur and chairman of Ashoka

To align the members of your leadership team, you have to invite them into the transformation process. They need to know they are being listened to. You have to respect them and their opinions and find out what they know. But if your leaders are dead weight on your change initiative, they must not be allowed to continue working with your staff—they can do a lot of damage.

If you are going to force transformation on any group, it should be your leadership team. If leaders are not ready to support essential change, perhaps your future organization is not the right place for them.

Alignment also means seeing how every part of the transformation touches other parts of the organization. For example, you may brand your customer service with behaviors that will reinforce your brand position and your marketing messages. But if no one aligns the hiring practices of Human Resources with the branded service initiative, every new staff member could lack the personality and behavioral style required to deliver your branded service. Many organizations, especially in the hospitality industry, have a policy of hiring "warm bodies." These warm bodies do not have a clue as to what their service should look like, and even if they did, they might not want to deliver it.

Lesson 2: Almost Everyone Resists Transformation and Change

New beginnings are often disguised as painful endings.
—Lao Tzu, ancient Chinese philosopher and poet

Even the people who know that they need change will still resist it. People will fight for traditions they do not understand, that have grown useless, and that actually impede moving ahead. Someone once said to us, "I was afraid I would become someone I wouldn't recognize." Entire organizations share this fear.

Part of the difficulty with transformation is that something has to be given up. And some people will always be attached to what has to change. Another difficulty with transformation is that it introduces an entirely new level of uncertainty.

Employees evaluate change based on how much it directly impacts them. If organizational culture is defined as the mix of shared values and beliefs, then a shift in organizational culture is going to be disruptive for even those who desire it. In fact, if culture is the way things are done in an organization, then any attempt to change behavior is going to feel like a smack right in the face of the culture. This means everyone is affected.

Lesson 3: Because Transformation Is Disruptive, You Cannot Just Tell People to Change

Reorganization to me is shuffling boxes, moving boxes around. Transformation means that you're really fundamentally changing the way the organization thinks, the way it responds, the way it leads. It's a lot more than just playing with boxes.
—Louis V. Gerstner, Jr., former chairman of IBM

You cannot push people faster on a transformation path than they are willing to go. Well, you can try, but you are not likely to be successful if you do that. We have learned that most people will accept transformation if you invite them into the process, respect their resistance, and listen to what they have to say. Many times, if you give them a chance to talk, they will talk themselves into changing.

When TMI International had to deal with new ownership about fifteen years ago, the new leaders went around the globe and listened intently to every licensee. TMI partners had a lot to get off their collective chests. Once the partners had a chance to vigorously voice their dissatisfaction, that negative baggage was gone. Energy moved quickly in a positive direction after that listening tour.

If you just attempt to order people to transform, they get extremely creative in figuring out ways to say "yes," when they absolutely mean "no." Sabotage goes underground. Whisper campaigns destroy anything positive that is happening.

Lesson 4: The Reasons for the Change Have to Be Communicated Honestly

Change the way you look at things, and the things you look at change.
—Wayne Dyer, best-selling author

Many resisters of change are convinced that the benefits gained from changing are fewer than the disadvantages that will occur if changes are not made. For this reason, tell your staff why the change is essential—whether it is to increase market share or to avoid having the market walk away from you. And if the reason is to increase market share, then staff members need to know the consequences of not attempting to do that.

Sometimes bad news gets people moving. If they do not know the reality of their situation, however, it is hard to convince them that they should change.

Lesson 5: The Way That You Communicate about Upcoming Changes Is Critical

The point of theatre is transformation: to make an extraordinary event out of ordinary material right in front of an audience's eyes. Where the germ of the idea came from is pretty much irrelevant. What matters to every theatre maker I know is speaking clearly to the audience "right now."
—Lee Hall, English playwright of *Billy Elliot*

Many executives craft their decisions in secrecy and then spring them on staff. Sometimes employees learn about changes that personally affect them through the media. Or they may wake up to see an e-mail announcing that two divisions are gone or get a recorded telephone message sent to everyone in the company announcing a drastic change.

The high degree of uncertainty and anxiety unleashed through this damaging style of communication is difficult to overcome. While a transformation process is taking place, business activities must go on. But if people are busy taking care of their emotional needs, productivity can erode to such a degree that it dooms the company. We have seen this happen more than once.

While communicating your reasons for change, you want to be careful to honor the past. Remember that the people who will be a part of your future change had their feet firmly planted in past activities. Let them know that they were not wrong or stupid to be doing what they did; however, things need to change.

People who communicate the change (normally, so-called leaders!) must be believable and respected. If your people suspect that you have hidden motives for creating change, no significant transformation will be accepted. For example, a hidden motive could include preparing to move all jobs in a certain category overseas in a couple of years. Employees may know the leaders are going to do this, but they are not talking about it at the moment. Under these circumstances, the next person who wants to make a change is going to have a difficult time overcoming this level of distrust. Employees will second-guess leaders every step of the way and never pour their enthusiasm into any transformation process. And their enthusiasm is critical.

Lesson 6: Listening to Disgruntled Employees Helps Heal Past Wounds

Transformation is a process, and as life happens there are tons of ups and downs. It's a journey of discovery—there are moments on mountaintops and moments in deep valleys of despair.

—Rick Warren, best-selling author

Asking questions gives people a chance to speak up. If they do not have an opportunity to say what is on their minds and talk about what they are feeling, they are likely to resort to the resistance mantra of "We've tried that before. It didn't work. If we just sit tight, we'll ride out this crazy idea as well."

When people think like that, it is clear they have not been welcomed into the change process and that the people driving the change do not understand how employees were affected during past change efforts.

Lesson 7: Almost All Change Efforts Result in More Work for Everyone—at Least for a While

> *Sometimes, counter-intuitively, it's easier to make a major change than a minor change. When a habit is changing very gradually, we may lose interest, give way under stress, or dismiss the change as insignificant. There's an excitement and an energy that comes from a big transformation, and that helps to create a habit.*

—Gretchen Rubin, author, lawyer, and blogger of *The Happiness Project*

Because of increased workloads that result from transformation projects, it is a good idea to get people involved in the change. Passions play a strong role here. If people are positively passionate about the proposed changes, they will approach the process with a burst of extra energy. Working with external consultants who know how to manage large-scale organizational changes is a good idea. They can take the burden of extra work off the shoulders of the existing staff. Your external consultants, with their "outside eyes," can also help you position your change so people get excited about it.

Employees may have to do things in new ways. This is where training can be helpful, whether it is technical training or soft-skills training. Many managers would love to be involved with the transformed organization but know that their old leadership methods will no longer work. They know they need help, so provide it to them.

Because transformation requires more effort, it is a good idea to not change everything at once. But definitely let people see how the total initiative will be rolled out. Proposed changes need to be talked about this way: "First we'll do this, and then after we are comfortable with that, we'll do this." You will never teach beginning swimmers to properly execute the butterfly stroke if you expect them to do this the first day they jump into the pool. But you want to let those little swimmers see what someone like Michael Phelps can do so they keep their eyes focused on the future.

Lesson 8: You Must Craft a Sustainability Program That Will Run Parallel to Your Change Initiative

The only way you survive is you continuously transform into something else. It's this idea of continuous transformation that makes you an innovation company.
—Ginni Rometty, president and CEO of IBM

We have found that designing a beautiful change initiative is easy. People will fall in love with it, but that romantic attitude can be maintained for a few weeks or a few months at best. Habits eventually overtake good intentions for the future. Therefore, somebody needs to be in charge of sustainability, and that person needs to be strong and committed to the change.

Think about building a change program that has a parallel sustainability program whose sole purpose is to keep new behaviors in place. This is particularly important when you are making changes to customer service.

A sustainability program has to include clear, measurable goals. If those goals are met, people should be rewarded. If those goals are not met, people have to be held accountable. It is all part of sustainability.

We have included a set of transformational questions at the conclusion of each of the organizational examples. If you want to use this book to improve your own operation, these questions should start you on that path.

Good luck! And have fun with your process. Life is way too short to make this type of work arduous. Remember, it is transformative!

PART I

Firing Up Passions

Be prepared for skeptics in any change process. Their questions will focus on valid questions, such as, What's in it for me? Why are we doing this? and Past change processes have come to nothing, so how is this change going to be any different? These are all valid questions and typically precede passion for the proposed change.

At the heart of successful organizational transformation processes is individual transformation. For individual transformation to take place, passions must be fired up for everyone in the organization. By helping people understand the *why* of the transformation, see the importance of their roles, and believe that the change is both possible and real, you can tap into the power of commitment. And with commitment, people can move organizational mountains.

Transforming Internal Service with an Organizational Mission

John Sabatino, CEO, TMI Australia

A key to transformation is asking the right questions of the right people. Some of these questions are remarkably simple, but until people consider them, they resist change. Such questions include, Who are our customers and what do they think of us? What does good service look like? Why are we here? What is our purpose? When you ask these questions and enroll people in the process and take action, change can happen.

Change was afoot. An edict from the Australian government was about to modify funding for universities. Higher levels of government financial support would, among other things, be contingent upon how many students they could attract. Money talks. Therefore, Australian universities began to consider how to become more attractive to potential students.

The vice chancellor of one of Australia's most esteemed universities believed that a businesslike, customer-centered approach could differentiate his university from other universities. He suggested that employees start focusing on their customers within the university itself. In other words, if internal departments treated other departments like valued customers, these customers would be able to stay focused on their most important job—serving and attracting students. The vice chancellor was confident this approach would work for the university.

The university would attract more students in general and reap additional financial benefits by becoming more attractive to foreign students, who paid higher tuition fees. Furthermore, because of the increased number of students, the university would receive higher levels of funding as directed by the Australian government.

The Test Case

With this in mind, TMI Australia was asked to work with the university's Finance Department. It was widely thought that the most challenging department in the university to transform was Finance. It was to be the test case.

If the Finance Department could transform its orientation to the other departments it served, perhaps the entire university would become more customer centered. Employees in other departments (in particular, the faculties) would spend less time on administrative financial matters. They would thus have more time to focus on teaching and research, as well as those valuable foreign students. All this could happen by transforming the customer consciousness of the Finance Department.

Many times transformation projects begin with a poke at one part of an organization. Such was the case here. The logic is solid. Changes initiated in one department can have an impact that becomes organization-wide. This is particularly true with a department like Finance as it had tentacles touching every other department and its faculty.

Many times transformation projects begin with a poke at one part of an organization… Changes initiated in one department can have an impact that becomes organization-wide.

The first step was to assess the internal relationships between Finance and other departments. What did the Finance Department's internal customers think about the service they received from Finance? TMI uncovered a clear and verifiable picture after conducting internal culture surveys, focus groups, and one-on-one interviews.

The news was not good. Other departments described an inability to understand Finance's budgetary process guidelines. They typically received arrogant reactions when they asked questions or requested help. So many departments ended up working on their own rather than turning to Finance for help. All this led to anxiety and confusion—and greater distance from Finance.

The result was, quarter after quarter, that departmental budgets were rarely met. It was not an overstatement to say that relationships with Finance got in the way of accomplishing financial requirements. One of the major schools in the university had such a poor relationship with Finance that the dean of this school regularly voiced his displeasure to the vice chancellor.

Departments wanted consulting help from Finance, but Finance thought it should offer a different type of help. The existence of this disconnect was established after just a few surveys and interviews. Many organization executives do not see the elephant in the room that is obvious to external consultants. Consultants come in with just a few questions that they keep asking again and again. They listen to informal conversations, those heard around water coolers. Even if everyone already sees the elephant, such as with this university, outside consultants are able to hear both sides of the story. They hear the attacks and they hear the defensive reactions.

The Challenge of Alignment

Once TMI consultants identified the problem, they needed to assess how willing the Finance Department's leadership was to change its behaviors and whether Finance employees had the necessary skills to do this. The answers to these questions revealed more challenges. Yes, the leaders in the Finance Department wanted change. They also did not like the animosity that existed between Finance and other departments. But the story they had created to justify their behaviors got in the way of their seeing a path to transformation.

People who worked in the Finance Department had different objectives than those of the university. The university promoted a mission that was twofold: provide students with world-class teaching and undertake world-class research. The vice chancellor's office understood that all departments had to be in alignment to achieve these two goals. The

Finance Department was not aligned—although its leaders believed it was. Finance employees did not understand that their department's role in this vision was to provide information and support to all the other schools and departments.

Another way to understand the challenge is that Finance employees believed they were working *at* the university. They did not see themselves working *for* the university. Supporting cutting-edge research and enabling young minds with the best possible education were not the drivers for performance and achievement in this critical department. In fact, the university's mission felt far removed from the Finance Department.

> Another way to understand the challenge is that Finance employees believed they were working *at* the university. They did not see themselves working *for* the university.

Finance staff believed that they had their own job to do and that each of the university schools had separate objectives and functions. They were ships passing in the night as far as those in Finance saw it. The other departments believed that the finance function was an ancillary function. Finance was, in their views, designed to allow them to take advantage of the considerable mathematical, budgetary, and accounting skills Finance possessed. They did not see Finance as part of a total team that could help with their research and teaching objectives. The deeper TMI consultants drilled, the more obvious this disconnect was.

Finance Department members realized that their financial expertise was not replicated in other departments. But this belief led them to the conclusion that they should handle all financial issues. Rather than fostering cooperation between the departments, this attitude created an unspoken attitude of "I know better than you what needs to be done. So get out of the way and let us do our job." It did not matter what was happening, Finance staff knew best.

When Finance members provided budget advice, they did not check to see how much sense it made to other departments. Little wonder that "arrogant," "they do as they please," and "inflexible," were phrases used to describe the Finance Department. A dean of one of the schools said,

"They give you the budget forms and process—which, by the way, seems to be different every year—and when we tell them we don't understand why this is so different, we don't get an answer. Finally, just before the due date all hell breaks loose and they come in on their white horses telling us they have to do it themselves. If something isn't correct, then we should have thought about this before the eleventh hour!"

Unfortunately, this type of judgment of and response toward finance departments is common, whether in a university or a commercial enterprise. In this case, the government edict changing funding to the Australian university system spurred self-reflection.

The chief financial officer took in the feedback and committed to change. In fact, rather than digging into a more deeply defended position, he became a true champion of this cause. He said the voice of the customer would be heard and acted upon. This is not always the case with transformation projects of this type. Frequently consultants find themselves fighting the self-defended target audience every step of the way. This group was different.

TMI positioned its first approach with the Finance Department as "What Good Looks Like" meetings. The financial team created a storybook based on examples of when they had experienced great customer service throughout their lives and careers. They delved into questions such as, When service was great, what sort of things did people do for you? How did you feel about your interactions with that company or person? With this kind of service, how likely would you be to continue to support these businesses or people, and how loyal would you be?

From the components of these recalled stories, they were able to establish descriptions of behaviors they wanted to display. The Finance Department called these guiding parameters "Guiderails." They named each Guiderail and then defined what it meant specifically to the Finance Department:

- To connect—Engage in two-way communication.
- To be passionate—Get personally close to "customers."
- To walk the talk—Seek opportunities to talk with people in other departments.

- To engage in conversations, not simply communication—Develop active and regular communication.

It is one thing to have a vision of where you want to be. Sometimes this is the easiest part of transforming behaviors. It is another to have the necessary skills and commitment to achieve the objective. TMI consultants arranged a series of personal one-on-one sessions with each team leader within Finance. They determined what progress was necessary to bridge communication gaps. Based on 360-degree feedback, a leadership, mentoring, and coaching program was set up.

> *It is one thing to have a vision of where you want to be. . . . It is another to have the necessary skills and commitment to achieve the objective.*

Transparent Communication

Finance decided that nothing would happen without the whole university hearing about it. The department set up a Facebook page as well as a separate section on the university's Yammer site. It introduced weekly meetings and information memos with a *Goss from the Boss* blog. Since *goss* means something amazingly good, everyone read the information memos. More than just the Finance Department was interested in what was happening. The entire university administration monitored what was going on. Soon everyone was talking about what was taking place over in Finance. The water cooler conversations about Finance were definitely changing.

Emotional Transformation

As is the case with many finance departments, functional behaviors were strong but delivered with little emotional connection. The Finance Department still needed to see itself as a relevant part of the university's mission. The employees' emotional disconnect was the heart of the problem.

A brilliant idea was had. To bridge this gap, the university's leading research academics went to Finance to talk about research conducted in areas such as juvenile diabetes and leukemia. They made a subtle point: the better the Finance Department was at providing financial services, the more time researchers would have to engage in this important work.

In other words, when it delivered excellent customer service, Finance actually assisted in finding cures for tragic illnesses. Its work was no longer just about budgets, accounting, and mathematics. The researchers who spoke to the Finance Department appreciated the opportunity to talk about their life's work. The Finance team began to talk about needing to provide support to encourage the research and be part of the outcomes! TMI calls this a "positive job description."

The researchers' message resulted in the necessary emotional breakthrough for transformation and pushed motivation levels sky high. Many in the Finance Department said that even though they had worked at the university for many years, after listening to those lectures, for the first time they went home to their families to tell them about the important research the university was conducting. Their families, after all, did not want to hear about spreadsheets and budgets. Finance employees gained a strong sense of pride knowing that what they were doing helped the university achieve a higher goal. Some people in Finance said they almost felt as though they themselves were working with test tubes.

With motivation at a peak, TMI offered workshops that focused on living the values of the Guiderails. Finance employees put "meat on the bone," as they called the process, by creating performance metrics. They put up charts in the department so everyone could see what was happening.

Groups with Finance took responsibility for achieving a specific aspect contributing to the Guiderails. For example, "to connect," one group created a process of serving morning tea at other departments to determine how to better offer service from Finance. Another group displayed Guiderail posters around the department; even their e-mail signatures had Guiderail symbols. Yet another group monitored the plans, number of meetings, and supporting activities in an action plan. They made sure to achieve the targets they set. A steering group was set up to report to the CFO about their continuing progress.

> *Finance employees put "meat on the bone," as they called the process, by creating performance metrics. They put up charts in the department so everyone could see what was happening.*

Outcome

TMI's consulting team became obsessed with how to make these behaviors stick. TMI wanted these changes to become part of "the way we do things around here." The Finance Department member also expressed concerns about sustainability. The CFO thought that it would not be long before staff returned to their old habits. Finance team members themselves doubted their ability to stick with the changes. They said, "It's great as long as it lasts" and "At least this time they have kept us in the loop—but who knows for how long."

As a result, other changes were made that supported the transformation process, including the following:

- Holding a series of brown-bag lunch programs
- Adding evaluation items about culture and customer orientation to performance reviews
- Communicating changes through the internal social media, Yammer
- Creating YouTube-type clips for the university's internal website
- Posting video clips on the employee Facebook page

Looking back months later, the TMI Australia team concluded that the Guiderails have worked. Student customer satisfaction scores have continued to improve. Cooperation has been enhanced between departments.

Each member of the Finance Department now has a responsibility and a set routine to increase engagement with each department. Today, the budgeting process always engages the departments. Ongoing Finance Department groups have been able to continue to drive culture change. As a result, well after the CFO and the vice chancellor left the university, we can say that transformation has stuck!

In this case, transformation did not occur because the university repaired a lack of competency. After all, the Finance team had all the right credentials to perform their financial role. But they had little engagement with their customers. Transformation, in this case, meant the emergence of a changed culture. By finding their passion in what they do, team members in the transformed culture saw customers, both departments and students, as central to forward progress.

Transformational Questions

1. Do your less-engaged departments or employees understand your organization's mission and their link to it?
2. What is stopping your transformation: a lack of skills or a lack of emotional commitment?
3. What defensive positions are keeping your elephants in the room from being addressed?
4. When you have identified your path to transformation, what are you doing to make sure the process is sticky and sustainable?

CHAPTER 2

Reducing Churn by Transforming Complaint Handling

Cynthia Nolan, Senior Account Director, TMI US

Sometimes improved customer service requires a shift in mind-sets and not just the learning of new skills. This shift can occur with complaint handling. When service representatives do not automatically revert to a defensive position upon hearing a complaint, they can find passion in their work. When it happens, the transformation is exciting.

In the late 1980s, cell phones cost upwards of $3,000. Yet many people were willing to invest that much money to get the latest technology. Even though cost was not that much of an issue to this growing market of mobile telephone users, for that price tag these customers expected more than "normal" customer service. To keep customers who faced early-adopter technological problems, telecom companies forced subscribers to buy into stringent no-change contracts that cost a bundle to terminate.

During this period, TMI US was asked to work with the national customer retention manager of a major US cell phone provider needing transformation in a major way. Specifically, the leaders of this giant telecom knew their customers were handled with less than finesse when they threatened to cancel their contracts. The retention manager (RM) was a newly created position that had previously not existed in this company. It was essential to create a point person responsible to stop the hemorrhaging of customers.

The RM was given free rein to do what was necessary to improve the dismal retention numbers. In addition to figuring out how to reduce the numbers of customers who wanted to cancel, this manager was also charged with converting unhappy customers into loyal, raving fans. Not a small task!

Understanding the Problem

The RM decided her first step was to put on a headset and spend time at her corporate call center simply listening. She spent hours both hearing what upset customers had to say and learning how the company's customer reps dealt with them. Customers were upset because their bills were incorrect yet again, their phones didn't work, someone in the retail store was rude to them, their phones dropped too many calls, a cell tower was being placed near their home, their phone was irradiating them, prices were too high, or they didn't make all the calls listed on their invoices and they wanted credit for the incorrect bills.

Customers were frequently rude and impatient. They used four-letter words left and right, shouting at the customer care representatives. The situation was worse than the RM had expected. There had to be a way to convert this behavior toward a positive outcome. The RM also asked the representatives what they liked and did not like about their jobs. It did not take long for a huge floodlight to flash: help was desperately needed for the benefit of both the customers and the staff.

Customer care reps for the most part pushed back on rude customer reactions, saying things such as "Don't yell at me, sir; it's not my fault," "I'm going to hang up if you don't stop yelling ma'am," "Don't talk to me like that," "I am going to hang up on you now," "Sorry, it's our policy; there's nothing I can do," "No one else has ever complained about this before," "They don't pay me enough to take this kind of abuse," and "I only work here." Sometimes they just hung up on abrasive customers without saying a word, causing even angrier customers to call back to take out their frustration on yet another service representative.

The customers also pushed back when hearing defensive responses and demanded to speak to the reps' supervisor. The supervisors could not keep up with the volume of calls directed to them. Delays in being able to talk with a supervisor did not make the customers any happier.

Most of the customers who called in to cancel their accounts seemed surprised when the representative gladly took their cancellation order just to get them off the phone. No one asked for these customers' continuing business.

This dynamic made the customer care reps extremely unhappy people. They knew they were not doing what was expected of them to retain customers. They got headaches, had stomach pains, and were grumpy. They took this unhappiness home with them every day. Many of them could not sleep at night, running unpleasant conversations through their heads over and over again and figuring out a good retort to use the next time someone said something like that to them! They wanted to quit, and many were already looking for other jobs. It was a recipe for disaster. Passion was needed to change the situation.

Turning Complaining Customers into Raving Fans

TMI entered the picture when the RM went to a local bookstore to look for books on complaint handling. There she found *A Complaint Is a Gift*, a book coauthored by Janelle Barlow, president of TMI US. Attracted by the bright blue cover with its big red bow[1], as well as the title, the newly minted manager bought the book and read it that evening.

The telecom RM decided to partner with TMI to deliver a customized training program based on the book. Representatives who were on the phones every day

> *The leaders at the wireless company decided they needed a turned-on champion to deliver this message. It was not about just teaching a technique. To turn their customers into raving fans, the representatives needed an advocate who was highly passionate, and this RM was more than passionate.*

were offered a six-hour training program. The training was delivered as quickly as possible to all call center office personnel across the United States. It took about six months to complete this widespread initiative, with the RM delivering every one of the programs herself. The leaders at the wireless company decided they needed a turned-on champion to deliver this message. It was not about just teaching a technique. To turn their customers into raving fans, the representatives needed an advocate who was highly passionate, and this RM was more than passionate.

During their training session, customer care representatives were encouraged to talk about their own issues—from their point of view. The representatives were, in effect, complaining customers themselves who were in many cases about to leave the telecom company and get jobs elsewhere.

The response to the program was universally positive, mainly because it addressed specific needs and provided relevant explicit tools. All participants received a copy of *A Complaint Is a Gift* to provide ongoing inspiration and to keep the program fresh in their minds. They were also given a job aide to put on their desks right next to their computers. The job aide was a small card with one of the tools, the Gift Formula, spelled out. It turned out that after just a few calls, this reminder device was no longer needed.

Many representatives who had wanted to quit their jobs did not, and they told the RM so after the training. Prior to the session, they felt as if they had been thrown to angry wolves and given no tools with which to respond. After the program they knew they could do something that had a good chance of working. They were eager to get started.

Regardless of how angry or abusive customers were when they called, almost all of them had a shift in demeanor when they heard a representative say something like the following to them: "My goodness! Thank you very much for calling me today and letting us know about this issue. I appreciate your being so candid with me. It helps to know when things like this happen to our customers so that we can do something about it and hopefully prevent it from happening again. I am very sorry this happened to you, and I'm going to take care of this right away. I just need some quick additional information from you." Upon hearing this, most customers immediately cooled down. Many apologized, and almost all were ready to get down to the business of partnering with the representative to solve their issue.

At the end of the call, the representative asked, "Is there anything else I can do for you today? . . . No? Well, thank you for being a longtime customer of ours; we really appreciate your business." And these customers stayed with the telecom company. Prior to the training program, the call center reps rarely got to say these words. After the training, however, many of the customers even asked to speak to the supervisor on duty so they could talk about what a great job the representative had done!

The Benefits of Transformation

What does transformation look like in a call center environment like this?

Customer cancellations in the wireless industry are called "churn." It's a huge problem in this and other industries, even today. In the company discussed here, churn was cut in half after a six-month period. That is an astounding number. Why did it happen?

Employees were happier because they were taught how to defuse customer frustration and anger. The representatives could see their numbers improving on a weekly basis. This, in turn, equaled a better experience for the complaining customer. The result was a win-win situation for many customers who told the care rep at the end of the conversation, "I really am sorry that I yelled at you. You have been fantastic to deal with, and you are a great asset to this company." These words created a big boost of positive feedback for the care representative, who now felt even more confident when handling complaints. Customers were no longer seen as enemies who were ruining the rep's days. A partnership to solve problems was created with the customer.

That is transformation. Was the problem solved 100 percent? No. Some of the telecom customers continued to be very difficult to deal

> *Customers were no longer seen as enemies who were ruining the rep's days. A partnership to solve problems was created with the customer.*

with. It seems that yelling into the telephone is easier to do than yelling at someone in person. Slamming down the receiver or clicking off a cell phone is also easier for a representative to do than turning his or her back on a live person and walking away.

Transformation does not mean 100 percent success, as TMI constantly emphasizes. In fact, if transformation meant a 100 percent solution, there would be no challenge once the solution was implemented. Transformation means finding that balance between solutions that are possible and solutions that are challenging. Too much challenge, and people give up. No problems at all, and people become bored. Neither is good for staff retention.

Anecdotal examples neither prove the success nor prove the failure of a transformation process. You have to look at large-scale data over a period to evaluate the success of your change efforts. In this particular company, retention rates increased from 16 percent to 33 percent for those customers who called in to cancel their service contracts in the first six months after the A Complaint Is a Gift program was implemented. These remarkable figures had a phenomenal impact on the carrier's bottom line. Representatives also stayed in much higher percentages, the average number of calls handled per hour by representatives increased, and the average handling time decreased.

Transformation may not have been perfect, but it certainly beat the obvious alternative!

Transformational Questions

1. When you strategize about how to offer better customer service, do you also take into account what is happening to your service providers? How do you assess this impact?

2. Are the goals you set for "fixing" customer service issues reasonable? That is, do you demand perfection or movement toward a target?

3. How do you let your employees know how they are doing? Are they given measurement numbers they can see on a regular basis to mark their improvement?

4. Are your educators or trainers people who are highly skilled and also highly passionate about the transformative information they are teaching? Or do you think that any manager can do an equally effective job?

5. Do you partner with outside agencies that know their subject matter inside and out, or do you ask your training department to put together a training program based on what they find on the web? What is the impact, and what is the cost of doing everything in house?

CHAPTER 3

When People Are Passionate, Transformation Blooms

Elena Khodko, Deputy Director, TMI Ukraine

Resistance is an inevitable part of the change process. When a different approach is taken—appealing to underlying emotional needs, while main-taining practical relevance—resistance can turn into passion for change.

It was a gloomy autumn day. Two long years had passed since the start of the world economic crisis. Looking back now, it is easy to see the signs of economic distress that were already there. But in 2008, the financial crisis seemed to appear like a rare black swan, coming out of nowhere. The only industries that survived the meltdown in Ukraine were agriculture and information technology. All the other sectors were languishing and searching for at least minor signals of an economic recovery.

So in 2010, when TMI Ukraine received a call from Ukraine's leading metal-producing company, it felt like pure magic. This large company was looking for providers to implement a comprehensive development program for its top managers. It was a good sign for the economy and the Ukrainian training industry and a great opportunity for TMI.

The Client

Established more than seventy years ago, the company had been a major Ukrainian state-owned metal-producing enterprise. Its production process involved a complete manufacturing cycle, including ore mining and processing, a by-product coking, and actual metal manufacturing. The company was sold to a foreign multinational corporation, a large, modern, financially solid corporation. The new owner is a leading supplier of quality steel products. Its leaders believe in transformation.

The new owners accepted the Ukraine government's requirements for ownership, agreeing to maintain certain investments, levels of production, and levels of environmental safety. Until all the stipulations were fulfilled, the government would continue to control the company. The government, naturally, did not want the foreign operator to buy the company in the midst of the economic crisis and then shut it down while still owning its considerable assets.

This government-owned metallurgical company had been one of the largest manufacturing enterprises in operation during the Soviet period. It had huge scientific and technical potential. Its resources were considerable. With a different owner, a new period in the company had arrived. Not everyone saw this as positive: the existing management consisted primarily of those who had been part of the Soviet period. However, the new owners could not just fire them all.

In the face of the outdated leadership style, the government-mandated objectives were challenging for the new owners. Seeing no other alternative, they decided to roll out a management development program. The new owners were committed to work with Ukrainian providers for this program, even though they had not used external providers for developing their managers before.

They determined that the proposed large-scale changes would affect every aspect of the manufacturing structure and organization. The objectives of the development program were to

- Change the Soviet managerial approach
- Help leaders develop up-to-date management skills
- Lay the foundation for a new corporate culture that encouraged more efficient work
- Engage staff at higher levels

Passion and the Bidding Process

It was assumed that this development program would be divided among several suppliers. It was too big to risk with one supplier. With this in mind, TMI account managers identified three of six areas of the program where they would be stronger and more passionate than their competitors.

The assumption proved correct, and passion paid off. TMI was selected to develop a two-day module on change management. Training in change management could make a huge difference in the company's fundamental mind-set. However, this program would be the last one in the two-year management development program. So TMI would not deliver the module for a year and a half.

Life rarely provides so much time to get prepared! But the time was used wisely. Not only did TMI's managing director, Irina Gubar, focus on module design, she ultimately became the trainer for the change management phase of the project.

Passion Overcomes Resistance

At first, the managers expressed enormous resistance. Most of them considered training to be a waste of time and money. It was a sensitive issue, especially because many workers had lost their jobs. People calculated how many jobs could have been saved with the funds being used for this project. Once they began to see what training could do, however, they said it was a pity that such training and development hadn't happened earlier.

The major difficulties faced during implementation of the program included

- Resistance from staff at every level
- Unclear communication about the transformation objectives
- Lack of feedback
- Lack of financial and other resources
- Bureaucracy and inefficient methods for implementing change
- Conflict of interests among the company's departments

- Low competency of some staff who had retained their positions because there was little accountability under the Soviet management model
- Minimal involvement of the top management team in communicating the change with passion

One important group that helped shape the design of the management development program was the young people in the company. These people had not grown up under Soviet rule and wanted nothing to do with Soviet time principles, standards, and management ideas. They wanted to be inspired and to feel their efforts would make a difference. The younger generation had arrived.

The midlevel managers did not like the changes they saw coming at them. They acknowledged that the Soviet approach to management did not work, but that did not mean they welcomed change. Company leadership had only a vague idea how to overcome this resistance.

When it was time for the change management module, the participants had already been working for a year and a half with other training vendors. The managers were satiated with training. "Enough," many of them said. But because of the intense focus over a year and a half to develop the customized change module, the training unleashed a passionate response among the participants. The feedback was in: the change management module was one of the most useful in the entire two-year management development program.

When people feel passionate, you cannot predict what will happen. That passion, however, needs ignition. Irina Gubar wanted all the participants to see that their entire lives—not just their work lives—could be transformed by using the change management approaches.

During the three months that Irina facilitated the change management module, she learned how people used the content. As anticipated, many used the same techniques at home that they were being taught to use at work. For example, they helped their children go through difficult change situations. Learning that transformation ideas were applicable outside the work environment helped fuel their passion.

One of the managers was sixty years old. He had been working at the metallurgical company his entire life. His father, his grandfather, and his son also worked there. He said, "Your story about the single bagger and double bagger changed my life." (This TMI signature example involves grocery store employees. A "double bagger" is a person who makes a special effort to offer exceptional customer service while bagging groceries.) He continued, "I was afraid of getting a layoff notice because I am already of retirement age." His eyes glistened as he finished, "I thought that my life would be over if this happened. But now I am sure I will be able to apply all my knowledge and experience whatever I am doing. I am no longer afraid of retirement. Thank you for that."

As anticipated, many used the same techniques at home that they were being taught to use at work. For example, they helped their children go through difficult change situations. Learning that transformation ideas were applicable outside the work environment helped fuel their passion.

All the feedback received from the groups who went through the program was summarized. It was a beautiful display of positive emotions by the employees. Irina then requested a meeting with the CEO to talk about the transformation in attitudes. It was not easy to set up that meeting, but Irina persisted. This conversation was a turning point in her relationship with the company. Irina talked about the results of the training as if she were talking about her own company. The CEO could feel her passion and was amazed at the transformation that had taken place based on the report she shared. The employee comments were evidence of this change.

Irina explained that the managers' initial resistance was actually a plea for additional information. They did not know what was going on in the company. What was needed was complete and clear communication at all levels. At first, senior managers had a hard time accepting this idea, but they could see the passion in the people who had gone through the program.

Enthusiasm for Additional Training

TMI was asked to facilitate a second program that focused on improving safety at work. This was to be a global initiative for all the company's locations around the world. The company wanted its managers to ultimately facilitate the program. In this way, they could offer it to everyone who worked for the company in Ukraine.

With passion, Irina delivered the safety program. More and more managers wanted to learn how to use the new tool to change the company. Ultimately, there was intense competition among the company's managers to decide who got to deliver the programs.

This program was, in many ways, transformational for the participants. Safety was not heavily practiced in the Soviet period. Simple ideas like being careful going up and down the stairs had never been considered. Almost no one taped electrical cords to the floor. Rear-seat seatbelts in automobiles were never used. Many participants said that they had initially thought the safety ideas were too ridiculous even to speak about. But passion trumped the naysayers again. Enthusiasm for safety replaced the fear of being ridiculed by colleagues.

Machine shop managers faced even stronger resistance from their team members when introducing change. For example, workers did not want to start using new equipment because they feared failing the certification test. One of the machine shop managers asked the workers to make a list of all the differences between the new equipment and the old equipment. While making this list, they taught themselves everything they needed to know to pass the certification test. This approach to certification tests spread like wildfire through the whole company.

TMI was next asked to bid on developing and implementing a Foreman's Academy. At this point TMI knew exactly what was required, understood the possibilities, and respected the resistance.

TMI learned that leaders in the company believed nobody would want to change from the position of a worker to a foreman. There were significant drawbacks to being a foreman. (There was even greater resistance to getting foremen to move up to the next managerial level.)

Highly skilled workers (steel makers, blast-furnace operators, roller operators) did not want the position because foremen lost their worker benefits—for example, they could not retire as early. Financial compensation was not commensurate with the level of responsibility. The job allowed practically no time for family life or relaxation. Irregular working hours without weekends were common.

Everyone understood this was the most difficult transformation project to date. But again, passion triumphed over resistance. Enrollment in the Foreman's Academy was huge! Some graduates of the academy were excited about new opportunities and asked to complete the facilitator's program. They could see many internal projects in the company where they could use the skills they would learn.

TMI employed respect and passion to break through the resistance. The research phase included ten interviews and two focus groups with foremen, as well as direct observations. To be able to see these hard workers actually doing the work of metallurgy was exciting. (Not so exciting were 6:00 a.m. morning meetings!)

One of TMI's principles of transformation is this: ask a question and invite change.

One of TMI's principles of transformation is this: ask a question and invite change. The fifty-two foremen who participated in the focus groups were surprised when they were asked their opinions. No one had done so before. They liked the idea that their views would be taken into consideration when designing the Foreman's Academy.

Before a single training program was held, positive attitudes were already beginning to be shared. Workers wanted to be involved. More so, they wanted to be asked to be involved.

The first wave of employees attending the Foreman's Academy started when the country was going through the epochal events at Maidan Nezalezhnosti (Independence Square), the central square of Kiev, the capital of Ukraine. During this period, the people of Ukraine protested for and won an association with Europe. Viktor Yanukovych, who was strongly supported by Russia's president Vladimir Putin, resigned the presidency. Shortly after this, Russia entered Crimea and annexed it.

And then not much later, a Malaysian Airlines Boeing 777 airplane was shot down over Eastern Ukraine. Turmoil was everywhere.

The second wave of entrants to the Foreman's Academy started despite the unprecedented economic recession that hit Ukraine during the ongoing war with Russia. In the midst of continuing economic problems, the third wave of participants to the Foreman's Academy graduated by the end of 2015.

People became so passionate about attending the programs that many of them moved their vacations to be able to attend all the sessions. Perhaps learning something new helped them divert their thinking about the turmoil within Ukraine, but this behavior would have been unheard of during the Soviet period.

As part of the training, TMI taught participants how to write and deliver an elevator speech (a short statement that can be delivered in the time it takes to go from the ground floor in a building to a few floors up in an elevator). One participant was selected to go abroad for one week of training based on the elevator speech he delivered to the company's CEO.

Again, people used the content of these programs to change their private lives. One participant, after studying conflict management, managed to address a decades-long conflict with his father. The ice in their relationship started to melt. The participant said it would take a lot of time and effort to rebuild the relationship with his father, but now they were at least listening to each other. And this was exactly what was happening inside the company as well.

Even More Passion

These programs revealed enormous individual transformation in the attendees. Now when asked who their favorite audiences are, TMI Ukraine facilitators say "Foremen" without any hesitation. Passion breeds even more passion, and it is fun to be around.

The passion that was uncovered in this company resides latent or dormant in every organization or group. It is a matter of finding it to unleash the expanding possibilities of transformation.

Transformational Questions

1. When you develop content that needs to be taught for your transformation initiatives, how do you make sure that there is a parallel approach to put passion into the content?
2. How do you get the people who facilitate your communication programs focused on uncovering the passion in your employees?
3. How do you awaken the passion among your leadership team about your transformation programs so your leaders are as passionate as you want your employees to be?

CHAPTER 4

Chinese Children, Dreams, and Teamwork

Edmund Lai, Chairman, TMI China

Sometimes firing up passion is a powerful experience for groups engaged in transformation. This example involves Chinese children, bicycles, and dreams, as well as some teamwork thrown in the mix.

It was a muggy day, the final morning session of a five-day international meeting for TMI and TACK in Shanghai, China. These annual meetings are always exciting. People working in different countries have a chance to be with each other. For many TMI and TACK partners and consultants, this is the yearly opportunity to deepen and renew friendships they have established around the world.

Only a few people knew what was going to happen. Everyone else thought they were participating in a team-building exercise sponsored by TMI China and led by our TMI Mexico partners.

The Setup

About 170 people from around the world were divided into teams and sent to one of several covered piles spread around the floor of the big ballroom. Instructions were clearly given, repeated, and then gone over again.

First the groups were told to remove the cloth over the pile in front of them. What lay beneath was obviously an unassembled bicycle. The participants were told to assemble it—in forty-five minutes. Expert bicycle builders were spread around room. Each team could ask two questions, but the experts could not help build the bicycles. Everyone quickly assessed who was on his or her team. The lucky groups had Dutch and German members, both groups comfortable on bicycles and knowledgeable about assembling them.

These were not simple bicycles that many people had grown up with as children. These bicycles had hand brakes, wires that needed threading, and many small parts that belonged somewhere!

And so the groups started assembling. Basically, no one read the instructions that came with the bicycles until they ran into trouble. Most groups depended on people within the teams who knew at least a little about bicycles. Others just got in the way.

The forty-five minutes went by way too quickly. Nobody finished the project, but two teams were ahead of all the others. It was a fun exercise, and of course every team wanted to win.

The groups were then told to put the partially completed bicycles down and come back to the tables in the front of the room to discuss the exercise. Of course, everyone still thought that this was a team-building exercise, and most of the groups had failed pretty miserably.

People were asked about responsibility, a question that did not seem to fit the team-building exercise, but TMI is a company filled with people who are nonresistant participants. They discussed that question, guessing that it related to how they responsibly interact with each other. The group was asked to think about love and how it can be passed within and between groups. That was intriguing and seemed to wander away from bicycle assembly. But stranger things had happened at "TMI World Congresses," as the international meeting is called.

After the learning from the exercise was exhausted, the group was then told that this was just the beginning of the exercise. Lunch was next on the agenda and instructions were precise: be back in the room exactly on time. In the meantime, the experts would reassemble the bicycles to make sure they were solid and safe. When the group returned from lunch, something special would be happening with these bicycles.

That was even more intriguing. But still no one knew what was to happen.

The Surprise

Once the participants were back in the room after lunch, the facilitators of the exercise told everyone that they were going to meet some special children who lived in Shanghai.

The children, between six and ten, had very poor parents. Both parents had to work some distance away from where they lived. So during the week the children were cared for in government programs. On Sundays, the children got to see their parents. Because of their circumstances, these children had few opportunities.

This was the first time any of the children had been in the type of fancy hotel in which the meeting was held. They had never been in the urban part of Shanghai. Just being driven through the wealthy parts of Shanghai was a treat for them.

For an hour and a half over the lunch period, both Chinese caretakers and TMI facilitators worked with the children. They had been taken to a room decorated with balloons and provided a large supply of art materials. The children were asked to share their dreams by drawing them on paper. They were also asked to make thank-you cards. And they were given cookies and ice cream. They thought this was the party to which they had been invited. They did not know about the bicycles or what awaited them in the ballroom.

The children were then taken to the ballroom and welcomed. They came into the room, holding hands, to the wild applause of dozens of "foreigners." The little tots were stunned and mostly just stared, eyes wide open, not knowing what was happening. But the people who had worked with them began to get them relaxed. The TMI participants immediately made the connection to the bicycles, but the children, of course, did not know this yet. They thought that this was just more of their special party.

The children started to share their dreams. Their dreams were no different from the dreams children around the world have.

The children started to share their dreams in Mandarin with translations by their caretakers. Their dreams were no different from the dreams children around the world have. They wanted to be doctors, nurses, astronauts, dancers, artists, singers, and teachers. One child said he wanted to take care of his parents.

Many members of the TMI family were openly crying. One little girl asked if she could dance for the group. One child sang a Chinese song to us. Then the children were paired with one of the teams that had assembled a bicycle that morning. The newly reassembled bicycles were wheeled in.

It is difficult to describe the looks on the children's faces. At that point, none of them had yet figured out that the bicycles were theirs to keep. They thought they could play with the bicycles and that was enough. All the teams helped the children ride the bicycles. There was plenty of space outside the ballroom where they could ride on a big green lawn. None of them knew how to ride as this was their first bicycle, and they were beauties—brand new in bright blue, red, yellow, and green.

Through sign language, the TMI teams let the children know that they were giving the bicycles to them. They could take them back to their homes. One small child was quietly standing. He did not understand that this bicycle could possibly be his. One of the non-Chinese women in the group spoke enough Mandarin to tell him the bicycle was his. It is possible that the shock of seeing a foreigner speak Mandarin was more overwhelming than the message she gave him. Finally, he got on the bicycle. And you could see ownership take place.

This event, which some TMI partners have scheduled for their large corporate clients, does several things. It is a team-building exercise—at least it starts out that way.

Transformation takes many forms. This simple act . . . reminded them, at a deep level, of how seemingly little things can make a lifelong difference.

But it quickly turns into an experience of giving. This work was not about what TMI (or its corporate clients) does but about the children. It was a moment in time enabling passions to run wild. It was a chance to feel the power of sharing. And it was a gift back to the community.

Transformation takes many forms. This simple act of unconditional giving made a deep impact on the "givers"—the TMI team. It reminded them, at a deep level, of how seemingly little things can make a lifelong difference. For the children, the afternoon will leave an indelible impression on them about the kindness of their fellow human beings.

Everybody won. Everybody learned. Everybody experienced passion.

Transformational Questions

1. Is your group in need of an emotional moment to unleash the passions that are in every gathering of people? How might you go about achieving this?

2. How do you create an experience with your people completely outside their regular experience when attending group meetings?

3. How important is surprise in some transformational experiences? Can you build surprise into your meetings and gain something positive from the element of surprise?

4. What happens to learning and transformation when people are moved to tears and joy? How do they use these emotions in their work? Or, does an event like this simply stand by itself as a testimonial to what humans can achieve if they work as a team?

CHAPTER 5

Leading Quality from the Heart

Conor O'Connell, Managing Director, TMI Ireland

Organizational transformation, especially in an area such as quality, is largely driven at the personal level. Behavior changes can be accomplished with a few simple steps as long as they impact the emotions.

In 1992, a multinational company in the telecommunications industry was in the process of deploying an organization-wide TQM (total quality management) initiative. As a part of the rollout, TMI Ireland was contracted to run Personal Quality workshops across three sites for six hundred Irish employees.

The goal of the workshops was to complement the statistical and technical TQM processes already put in place by the company's Quality Management Department. The Personal Quality program was a success involving everyone from operators to engineers to salespeople. Everyone immediately began to use a shared language based on simple quality concepts. Compared to technical quality, the quality training was powerful, personal, and fun.

The Callback

Jump ahead twenty-two years later to 2014. The phone rang. "Hey, Conor, do you remember me? It's Kenneth here. I worked in the Quality Department when you consulted with us back in the early 1990s. Do you still do those quality workshops you did with us back then—you know, the AP-IP [Actual Performance–Ideal Performance] Model Parachute Packers, and Do-Check?"

Kenneth and Conor met soon after. When they had first met, Kenneth was a young quality manager. Twenty-two years later, he had less hair, more experience, and a much greater level of responsibility in the role of global quality vice president. Arriving at the site, Conor met the receptionist, who had attended the training many years earlier. She called Kenneth to exclaim, "It's the parachute guy." Those training messages were still strong more than two decades later.

Kenneth explained how the company was now a part of a bigger operation, employing around ten thousand people across four continents. The company specialized in telecommunications infrastructure. It now manufactured cables, antennae, radomes, and other high-end telecommunication products.

The quality stakes in Kenneth's department were high. He indicated that the team had done all the usual quality work, including standard operating procedures, corrective and preventive actions, statistical process control, Pareto principle analyses, and cause-and-effect analyses. What he felt was missing was the personal ownership and responsibility for quality.

Among his duties was the installation of highly sensitive equipment—cell phone antennae. These antennae are the tall boxes that are anchored to pylons or placed on the tops of buildings and are an essential part of the cell phone infrastructure. They have to be robust enough to withstand storms and poor weather while protecting internal equipment that is *very* sensitive and delicate: the incorrect sequence of tightening bolts can distort a signal. Moreover, if a unit fails or is installed incorrectly, cell phone service in the area goes down. Once a signal is lost, maintenance personnel have to climb the towers to fix the problem. The costs of failure are enormous.

The antennae were manufactured in a number of plants in China. Data showed that the assembly lines were operating at a 92.5 percent level of quality performance. In short, there was a 7.5 percent error or failure rate. The costs of repairs in terms of rework, customer dissatisfaction, compensation, scrap, opportunity cost, and reputation amounted to huge sums of money.

TMI's mandate was to reduce the error rate on the assembly lines by running a train-the-trainer process using TMI's Personal Quality training program with the Chinese quality team. They would then conduct training with assembly line workers.

The quality team had already adopted the traditional approaches to quality management. . . . But to achieve higher levels of quality, they needed to do things differently.

The quality team had already adopted the traditional approaches to quality management. They were good engineers with good hearts. But to achieve higher levels of quality, they needed to do things differently. Conor ran TMI's training for them in China and in Ireland over ten intensive days.

A New Way of Thinking about Quality

Imagine a training room filled with Chinese technicians. In front of them stood an Irishman whose mission was to shift their paradigms from focusing on quality techniques to focusing on people. Fortunately, the Chinese still revere their teachers!

The training began without resistance. The technicians were polite while they were told that there are five types of quality—company quality, service quality, product quality, team quality, and personal quality. They listened with increased interest when they were told that personal quality is at the heart of all the other types of quality. As the training program progressed, something happened. Their eyes lit up as they had aha moments. They started to see that quality was more than a "company thing."

You could feel energy in the room increase as these technicians realized the impact of poor quality, not from a technical viewpoint, but from a personal angle. They could relate to children who got sick from poor-quality food preparation. They all knew people who had gotten the wrong medication at a pharmacy. They knew what it felt like to have the wrong product delivered after they had ordered something online. They especially hated having to follow up on errors in their bank direct-debit accounts. Conor spoke about topics they did not anticipate covering in a quality training program and also examined what it takes to deliver "world-class quality." For example, what does the way that German farmers meticulously stack their firewood have to do with quality? The short answer is "a lot!"

If you drive through rural Germany, you will see neat piles of firewood stacked by every farmhouse. Every piece of wood is exactly the same length to fit the stoves that are used. Precise stacking allows the wood to weather and makes the pieces easy to handle. All the farms use exactly the same system. How did this happen? Knowledge has been passed from generation to generation. People's home upbringing has produced a culture of quality about stacked firewood in the German countryside.

The Chinese came to realize how their home upbringing had an enormous impact on their personal quality standards. Quality becomes a value and an attitude in early childhood. It is not a set of technical exercises; rather, it is a mind-set about how people do things and deliver for customers.

They had more aha moments when they set their own ideal performance levels. They realized that quality must, first and foremost, be inculcated into human behavior.

The quality managers came away with a new way of thinking. They went from focusing on the technical and sophisticated to adopting a simple and human approach to quality. They learned to listen to stories of personal quality in action in the workplace rather than to rely just on statistics.

> They went from focusing on the technical and sophisticated to adopting a simple and human approach to quality.

They shared some very powerful stories themselves that brought power and impact to the subject. They came away excited about the possibilities that this new way of thinking opened for their assembly-line employees.

Once the train-the-trainer sessions were completed, this group then trained about four thousand people across the plants in China. The impact was tangible and quick. People on the assembly line practiced human quality principles that they had been taught—how to be "parachute packers" (reliable team members) on the assembly line and how to "do-check" (i.e., always do your work and then check it for accuracy). The workers and teams measured their actual performance and ideal performance. Quality had moved from being the responsibility of the Quality Department to being owned by people on the line.

Of the twenty-two assembly lines that the group trained, sixteen are now achieving their targeted ideal performance levels. The failure rate has been reduced from 7.5 percent to just 2 percent. The investment in Personal Quality training was repaid a hundredfold, adding millions of dollars to the company's bottom line. When the celebrations about financial success were taking place in China, the operators pointed out that up until then quality was a distant and obscure concept. Now it was real and easy to understand. The killer ingredient was their involvement. All this was achieved through a change in mind-set, backed up by a common language that led to a change in specific quality behaviors.

The program went from strength to strength. Many more thousands of employees from this company have been trained in TMI's Personal Quality program in other parts of China, the United States, Germany, and Ireland. Quality has taken on a new meaning across the world, with a focus on people getting involved and taking responsibility to personally own quality performance.

This transformation did not end at the assembly line. Managers started to hear about the program. The next phase was to migrate the concepts and the training to other departments—Research and Development, Sales, Finance, Design, and Radio Engineering. Soon everyone began to talk about how mistakes and quality issues in other parts of the company cost the company enormous sums of money.

One idea that almost every manager has commented on—whether in the United States, Europe, Asia, or Africa—is that when it comes to quality, the same fundamental principles apply. If you want to transform quality in your organization, focus on your people. The human side of quality is a universal concept on a transformative path to success.

Transformational Questions

1. Is your transformation focus just on numbers and tangibles? If you focus on the human side of the equation, what impact will that have?

2. How can you make your transformation efforts relevant to the everyday lives—beyond the workplace—of your employees?

3. What are the small number of key concepts that you can use to transform the thinking and behaviors in your organization?

CHAPTER 6

Water Tanks and Passion

Sally-Ann Huson, Global Value Proposition Manager, TMI International

Sometimes the differences between employees and the customers they serve are so vast it seems that nothing will bridge the gap. Passion, however, can help the two groups reach across the divide, starting with something as simple as saving enough money for a water tank.

O nce there was a rounded hill covered in grass and trees in the valleys of Bophuthatswana and the distant Pilanesberg hills of South Africa. Now a mighty palace sits there, topped with ten domes that straddle high towers, the tallest one of which punches 70 meters (230 feet or about twenty-three stories) into the sky.

Work began on the Palace of the Lost City in August 1990. Over 1.75 million cubic meters (over 2 million cubic yards) of earth was moved. Mountains were created; tons of rock were blasted and concrete poured. All this work was done to accommodate over two hundred bricklayers who laid thirty million bricks. Craftspeople from all over the world helped put the luxurious finishing touches on the hotel and resort. Murals, marble, and magic all awaited visitors from around the world upon their arrival.

The rotunda in the Palace had a domed ceiling about eight stories above floor level with a span of almost 100 feet (29 meters). Construction of the unique marble mosaic floor in the rotunda involved laying almost three hundred thousand pieces of tile. Outside, a wave pool was installed with a surfing wave six feet tall that moved at about ten miles per hour onto a specially constructed beach. The largest manmade waterfall ever constructed both in volume and elevation—the Grotto—was part of the property. A newly designed and created eighteen-hole golf course would have live crocodiles in the water hazard at hole thirteen.

During the nineteen months of building, not only bricks and mortar were set in place. No fewer than five forests, from a baobab forest to a rainforest, were planted. Some of the trees were hundreds of years old. The sheer luxury of the interior of the Palace was designed by some of the best designers from the United States, the United Kingdom, and the Far East.

Such was the dream and vision of one man—Sol Kerzner. Given his previous hotel projects around the world, this South African born to Russian Jewish immigrants was planning the highest degree of luxury for every visitor for Sun City Resort, Sun International's flagship resort. Kerzner developed multiple hotels, resorts, and casinos around the world for the Sun International Group. Sun City Resort itself has four hotels, including the luxury Palace of the Lost City. TMI's role was to work with employees to create lasting memories for the resort's guests and customers. In this case, because of the wide divide between the staff, who were from mixed South African tribes, and managers, who were mostly white ex-patriates, the challenge was to get everyone to see that the Africans were capable of providing the highest levels of service in keeping with the property. This was more than a small challenge— almost everyone involved did not see how this could possibly happen.

The Background and Political Landscape of the Time

In February 1990, President F. W. de Klerk announced Nelson Mandela's release from prison after twenty-seven years of incarceration, eighteen of which were spent on the two-square-mile rocky outcrop of Robben Island. President de Klerk lifted the ban on the African National Congress, as well as other antiapartheid organizations. The slow dismantling of the apartheid system followed, with laws being changed and restrictions lifted over several years.

Until this time, institutionalized racism, the legacy of apartheid, tribalism, nepotism, and the South African government's stance on gaming had created a turbulent melting pot of uncertainty for resorts like the Palace. Once Nelson Mandela was released, the first democratic elections were announced and held. Mandela was voted in as the new South African president in May of that same year. This political appointment generated an air of excitement, hope, expectation, racial reconciliation, and forgiveness.

The new government shifted its policy on gaming, which up until this time was not permitted within South African boundaries. But the restrictions were gone, and this left the Sun International properties (twenty-six sites in all), including Sun City Resorts outside the borders of South Africa. This meant that Sun City Resorts' value proposition had to shift. No longer could the company expect customers to travel to its venues some distance away when they could now go to newly created and official gaming venues that were springing up much nearer to South Africa's population centers and international airports.

TMI's Work

In late 1992 TMI UK was invited to work with the Sun International group to help it deal with the massive shift in the gaming industry. TMI key account and business development managers met with members of Sun International's senior leadership team. These were individuals who had opened and run some of the most successful hotel, resort, and gaming operations in the world.

The Sun leadership team explained their situation. They recognized they now had to compete for their customers. They were making huge investments in renovations, attractions, and entertainment to continue to draw people to their properties. Their dilemma was what customers experienced once they got to these magnificent properties, such as the Palace.

Guests saw service providers who were, in their perception, often rude and sullen. The staff seemed to have very poor standards of service with little ability or motivation to resolve problems. Guests put up with the problem so they could stay at one of the luxurious properties and spend time at its casinos. After all, previously there were no casinos within South Africa. If guests complained too much, they risked being asked to leave—unless, of course, they were "whales," high rollers in gaming terms.

Another issue concerned the attractiveness of the venues to international guests. The high rollers wanted more than just gaming opportunities. They wanted to have a great experience while on the property, particularly if their families were with them. They wanted international service standards comparable to or better than those of other properties they visited across the globe because of the distances they had to travel. Finally, the grand architecture and luxurious surroundings raised their expectations of what their service experience should be.

Most of the people working at the property lived off site in nearby townships. Africans were confined to specific residential areas while they worked at jobs serving only whites. The townships had little in the way of luxury. Indeed, water was delivered every week to the communal water tank, and the power supply was intermittent and heavily restricted. If life at home meant living in one of these townships for blacks only, imagine the disconnect when working at a property like the Palace where there were five swimming pools, running water, and regular power.

International cultural differences were also an issue. Respect for elders meant keeping one's eyes downcast to appear submissive and servile and certainly not smiling. On the positive side, everyone was given three new uniforms to wear, which were all laundered by the on-site laundry. The uniforms became a source of pride to those who until then had a very limited work wardrobe. Showers and cleaning products were provided for all employees, and for many, taking a warm daily shower was a rare treat.

The materials provided to TMI workshop participants were treated with reverence as few people could afford anything in a printed format, other than perhaps a secondhand daily paper shared within their community. Here they received a fresh copy of a new book that was their personal property. The workbooks were used to teach others in their townships, passing on the stories and lessons learned from attending the programs. The workbooks were written in a way that took into account the high levels of illiteracy. They were designed so that everyone could use the materials whatever their reading or language capability and keep their dignity intact.

In the various South African languages used among the workers, there were no comparable words or concepts for things like *goals* or *profit*. For example, at a Sun property in Mmabatho, one worker said she wanted to own her own water tank. This is understandable given that the communal tank was empty most of the time. It was filled only on a weekly basis. No one had a say about how people used the water from the communal service, so by the end of the week everyone suffered from a lack of drinking water.

The TMI consultants found ways to use colloquial terms to reinforce key messages that at times were contrary to the workers' beliefs, upbringing, and culture. The concept and discipline of doing something small but doing it regularly was explained to the group as a means of achieving goals. So by doing something small every day, this woman could eventually get to her goal. The woman, in her late forties, looked as though she were in her late fifties. She had lived a hard life. She worked on the resort property as a room attendant and supported her family as the breadwinner. There was little extra cash at the end of each week. She mentioned picking up a few extra South African rand left in the rooms by guests who would empty their pockets of the coins they no longer needed when going back to their homes overseas. The TMI facilitator showed her how her water tank goal could be

> The workbooks were written in a way that took into account the high levels of illiteracy. They were designed so that everyone could use the materials whatever their reading or language capability and keep their dignity intact.

achieved. He demonstrated how saving a few rand every day for almost a year would give her enough savings to buy her water tank.

During the break she came up to the facilitator and said, "This is all well and good, but how do I do it? If I keep the money in my pocket I will spend it; if I keep it at my place it will be taken." The facilitator took her to the on-site bank. He explained to the manager and cashier what they wanted, and they agreed to her special and very specific actions. The woman was given a savings bankbook and every day she placed a few coins into her account. She even traveled to the property on weekends to add to her bankbook.

When the TMI facilitator returned to that resort a few months later, the first person who ran up the driveway to greet him was the woman. She waved her bankbook at him and very proudly showed him that every day she had placed coins into her account and that she now had more money than she had ever had in her entire life. Did she get her water tank? TMI suspects she did. One thing for sure is that she had put herself in a position of choice, a place she had rarely ever been in during her hard-lived life. Her example served as a passion point for the rest of the employees and, indeed, for other TMI participants worldwide as her story has been retold many times.

> *She had put herself in a position of choice, a place she had rarely ever been in during her hard-lived life. Her example served as a passion point for the rest of the employees.*

More examples like this emerged as TMI worked across the Sun group. TMI facilitators heard that as people were bused to the hotels to attend the workshops, many were threatened with physical harm. Because they had jobs, they were seen as robbery targets. This was the first time in their lives many of them had been invited to participate in seminars where they learned skills and developed attitudes that made their lives enjoyable. As a result, they stood up to the threats and made it to the workshops.

A Managerial Transformation Begins

Africans on the property were not the only ones who began to believe in themselves. While most members of the leadership team had operated other properties, few had experience in running successful Sun properties. Part of the issue was that there was no common view about what Sun International stood for and how it would differentiate itself beyond its amazing physical structures.

TMI's work began by using traditional tools (focus groups, interviews, and a culture survey) to assess how the leadership team felt about their performance. The idea was to make visible the invisible and to deal with the facts as they were found. This began a series of planning workshops with leadership teams across all the Sun properties. Where did they want to be, and how could they get there? Service concepts were introduced. These concepts were needed to encourage, support, and motivate both management teams and other employees on the properties. The leaders, to a person, had extremely low expectations about the potential and capability of their employees.

Based on these discussions and the output, the UK team designed a two-day workshop that everyone, including the leaders and managers, working at all twenty-six properties would attend. Each workshop was to be opened by the hotel or the property manager.

In the two-day program, experiential learning was emphasized. This was essential because most of the employees were illiterate. TMI was asked to remove the experiential exercises because, as the leadership said, "They would be too hard for people to understand." Having used variations of these exercises all over the world, TMI facilitators knew they could make this type of learning work. In fact, experiential learning was the only way the concepts would stick.

Gone was the idea that they had to work to the lowest common denominator. High expectations led to higher levels of service delivery.

TMI agreed to meet the leaders' demands—after a pilot. If this style of learning did not work, the exercises would be removed. Of course, all the exercises stayed in the workshops and, in fact, became the most popular content. The local Africans attending were proud to show their managers what they could do. Indeed, some were better at doing the exercises than many of their managers!

This transformational shift in thinking for managers was a key part of the organization's continued success. Gone was the idea that they had to work to the lowest common denominator. High expectations led to higher levels of service delivery. Discussions about customers and their experiences and how systems could be changed to make it easier to deliver better service opened up a new mind-set for many.

Parameters were established to monitor and measure service behaviors. As a result, the resorts went from strength to strength. People were passionate about creating a positive service experience for the resorts' guests. Many of the managers who were in place in the 1990s are still with the Sun properties.

If managers and leaders believe that people are incapable of doing the task at hand (in this case, delivering friendly, engaging, and high levels of service), then that belief becomes the reality. But if this belief can be changed both in the minds of the leaders and in the minds of employees, transformation is well on its way.

Transformational Questions

1. Are there mind-sets or sets of assumptions about members of your teams that could erect barriers to your transformational journey?

2. What are the managerial and staff routines that must happen every day to move you forward on your transformational journey?

3. What is your transformational "water tank"? How and when will you achieve this goal?

4. What external changes do you anticipate will affect your business model? How can you transform your teams to be in a position of strength if those changes happen?

PART II

Aligning Your Leadership Team

All eyes are on the boss. The behavior of leaders and managers—what they do and what they do not do—sends strong signals to their teams. Employees throughout the organization will mimic their behavior—positive, negative, or passive.

Different levels of the leadership team play different roles during an organizational transformation process. Senior leaders need to be aligned—holding the same picture of the future and how to get there. It is critical that they demonstrate to employees, through their actions and their words, that they are committed to the change.

Transformation processes need to be designed so that managers take ownership of the change among their own teams. And for the transformation to take root in the organization, teams need to understand and collaborate with each other. Relationships of mutual understanding and support need to be built between managers of different departments.

CHAPTER 7

Leading Change from the Top

George Aveling, CEO, TMI Malaysia

Senior leaders play an important role in transformation projects, but they may not appreciate the impact of their presence—or absence—during events and among employees in the workplace. One way to have them appreciate the power of their presence is to orchestrate for it to happen. Once senior leaders see and feel the impact of their physical presence, belief in and commitment to further action will follow.

Picture this. The CEO of TMI Malaysia is at a business networking function. He takes a drink offered to him and turns around to see a friendly, open face. The two men smile at each other and exchange business cards. It's a normal exchange at a networking event except the second man looks at the TMI Malaysia card he has just been given and says, "TMI! Time Manager International!"

"That's right!" replies George Aveling, the CEO of TMI Malaysia.

"British Airways!" the gentleman continues.

"I am impressed!" George exults.

"Putting People First!" the gentleman says excitedly.

"Now I am really impressed!" whoops George.

That was the opening volley in a major TMI transformation project. The gentleman was the deputy CEO of the local arm of an international bank.

The bank was actually in good shape. But while it had been growing its market share, it also wanted to develop a more sustainable customer relationship approach that would align with a planned transformation of its systems and service culture. Its aspiration was to be "Malaysia's Most Preferred Bank."

People within the bank were attracted to the idea of delivering "branded customer service" that was unique to the bank. This phrase also happened to be the title of the book written by TMI partners Dr. Janelle Barlow, TMI USA, and Paul Stewart, TMI New Zealand.[1] Someone within the bank had read the book.

"We have a big brand. But we don't have a branded customer experience," said one of the senior leadership team at a later meeting. TMI Malaysia brought in colleagues from New Zealand to partner on what would be an incredible two-and-a-half-year journey to embed a branded customer experience in the organization.

Getting Senior Team Buy-In

Fast-forward a few months after the networking function. The bank agreed to the first phase of the branded customer service journey—a two-day leadership-planning meeting. As a critical first step to achieve alignment, the bank's top twelve executives attended the off-site meeting.

In any organizational change process, it is important to engage the senior leadership team. Without solid support at the senior level, change efforts become like houses of cards. They fall apart, sometimes quickly, sometimes slowly. But they do fall apart!

Without solid support at the senior level, change efforts become like houses of cards. They fall apart, sometimes quickly, sometimes slowly. But they do fall apart!

The workshop started very smoothly. TMI introduced the concept of branded customer service and the thinking and philosophies of Appreciative Inquiry, a process that focuses on what is working instead of what is not working. TMI consultants ran a Future-Backwards exercise to help the executive team develop a clear picture of the bank that they wanted to create while understanding where the bank was at the time. For transformation processes to be successful, all members of the senior team need to see the same picture of the past, the present, and the future. Energy in the room grew as the picture became clearer to the team.

And then the executives were asked to participate in a right-brain drawing activity to design the bank's branded customer experience. All of a sudden, things got emotional. One senior executive felt that part of the group was not taking the exercise seriously. The situation was tense for a little while as he asked some hard questions. "Do you really believe that your diagram represents what our bank's customer experience should be?" he asked in an assertive and annoyed voice. This was not exactly an Appreciative Inquiry type of question.

Frequently, emotional outbursts of this type either unify the team or stop the process. In this case a breakthrough was achieved. This marked the beginning of the emotional buy-in of the senior team to the branded customer experience. However, they were unable to complete the definition of the bank's branded customer experience at the two-day workshop. Too many of the bank's leadership team had sharply divergent views about what that experience would look like—at that moment.

After some debate at a subsequent meeting in the bank's headquarters, they were able to arrive at a consensus. The foundation for the delivery of the bank's branded customer service had been determined. A number of members of the senior team—but not all—totally bought in. But there is more to leading a change process than just buying in at an emotional level.

The Power of Presence

Fast-forward again to the first event with fifty leaders who would be major change agents for the initiative. Members of the executive leadership team were asked to drop by during this three-day event. When company executives participate in initial transformation activities, it sends powerful signals of their commitment to and support for the process.

Sure enough, on the first day of the event, a few members dropped by. Most of them stayed at the back of the room. They seemed rather uncomfortable, saying, "What difference does my presence make?"

Little did they know! It made an enormous impact on employees that their executive team took the time to join them.

One of the leaders was asked to speak to the group. He said a few words and the group responded with more than enthusiastic applause.

The executive immediately saw the power of his presence to energize the bank's management team and to energize the process. People still talk about this memorable moment years after the event.

The Power of Connection

That night, the executives learned about the power of connection in large-scale organizational transformations. A great deal of planning had gone into preparing for a social function at a restaurant that would dramatize the bank's desired customer experience. TMI calls this a "Brand at a Party"; it is a powerful way for a leadership team to show their alignment with what they expect. It also creates a memorable event, exemplifying what they want to see in their service delivery.

Imagine the end of the first day of the workshop. Everyone was a little tired, but all the participants headed to the lobby of the hotel and waited for a bus to take them to an end-of-first-day dinner. Two buses arrived and stopped in front of the hotel. The bus doors opened and members of the executive team hopped off and welcomed the fifty managers on board! One of them happened to be the CEO. As the buses left the hotel, the CEO and other top bank leaders handed out refreshing towels to the passengers and greeted each one individually.

The group was stunned. People whispered to each other, "What is happening here? This has not happened before. Management must be serious."

The senior team got another taste of the power of connection at a human level with their colleagues, of going that extra step to excite them, to create a "wow!" experience.

The bus stopped in front of a restaurant where the evening meal would be shared together. The fifty managers were welcomed at the door by more members of the top team. The managers were recognized and treated as individuals throughout the evening as if they had been invited to a party. Everything was done to make them feel like special guests. They now could appreciate what the bank's branded customer experience should feel like. And the senior team got another taste of the power of connection at a human level with their colleagues, of going that extra step to excite them, to create a "wow!" experience. Change was starting to happen at many levels!

Engagement as Usual

Now jump ahead two years. By then, TMI had helped the bank navigate through an organization-wide branded customer experience transformation process. After creating branded customer experiences for their managers at a number of events, senior management had learned a new, powerful leadership behavior—engaging and connecting when any significant change is proposed.

Leaders in the bank also took part in an induction program for a new banking subsidiary. The participants were new recruits. At the end of the first day, the recruits left the meeting room at 5:00 p.m. and were asked to return in exactly fifteen minutes. The doors opened at 5:15 sharp. When the participants reentered the room, an honor guard greeted them. It consisted of the members of the bank's senior leadership team, including the CEO.

This senior team, showing a high degree of alignment, excitedly embraced their next role for the evening. They served trays of finger foods to the fifty somewhat surprised and very delighted new recruits, exemplifying the meaning of the word *service*.

The mind-set of the senior team had shifted and the leaders said it was "pretty obvious" that this type of engagement makes a big difference—and is a natural part of the process of leading change. The lesson had transferred over from TMI's initial experience with the bank. The senior leadership team had gone from "I can't see the point of my being here" to "My presence, even for a short time, is important to my role as a leader of change in this organization."

Only a tiny portion of the total bankwide transformation process has been shared here. But transformation of the senior team from a powerful but less-than-aligned group into an aligned force to create change was an important piece of this very successful transformation process.

The bank successfully created a customer experience that supports its unique style of branded service. In the process, it achieved its targets in terms of employee engagement, customer recommendation, and revenue.

Transformational Questions

1. How can you get your senior executive team to be willing to do what is necessary to stand behind your transformation project?

2. If the members of your senior team do not appreciate the power they bring to your change initiatives, how can you enroll them to publicly stand with you?

3. How can you ensure all members of your senior team have the same picture of the change experience you want your organization to make?

4. As a part of your transformation process, what is your strategy to use senior management alignment and commitment to touch every part of your change initiative?

CHAPTER 8

When Having Great Departments Is No Longer Enough

Cynthia Nolan, Senior Account Director, TMI US

Simple transformational strategies can have enormous impact. Sometimes all that's needed is to bring together people from different parts of the organization. The building of strong relationships and an appreciation of each other's issues are potent levers to major improvements in service quality.

Improving your customers' experience when you are at the top of your game is a challenge. In situations like this, transformation can be incremental and still be worth pursuing. Transformation does not have to be earthshaking.

Our cruise line client, the star of this story, considers itself to be the best of the best in its particular niche of the market. The company has an exceptional reputation. Many guests come back year after year after year for yet another cruising experience. People love the excursions, their staff, the staterooms, the service, the food, and the ships.

Improving a Reputation for Excellence

The cruise line's leaders have never been satisfied with just being the best. They want to continue to improve in this competitive industry. This approach is clearly working for them in terms of increasing revenues and a growing market share. It is exciting to be around this kind of energy.

TMI has worked with the company for some time, looking for ways to help its leadership teams create better customer experiences. The company already has a high standard for customer service and it typically meets or exceeds that standard. So the system and the customer service approach do not have to be reinvented. But service levels can still be improved by tweaking something that may have been overlooked.

The departments in this cruise line, as in most hospitality companies, are silo oriented. As the leaders have said about themselves, "We work in silos with blinders on about the other silos."

> *The company already has a high standard for customer service and it typically meets or exceeds that standard. . . . But service levels can still be improved by tweaking something that may have been overlooked.*

But customers do not see a ship's departments as separate entities. They experience all service as a totality, and when one department gives incorrect information about another department, customers get confused. Customers, as the saying goes, do not understand why the left hand does not know what the right hand is doing. It is not enough for every department to offer great service. When customers feel like service starts and stops at a department's boundary, they judge that as bad service.

This client asked for help in developing and offering a program on how to lead the service experience. It wanted department-by-department offerings for all the managers of this cruise line—for example, hotel managers, executive chefs, sous chefs, maître d's, program directors, and concierge managers. Instead, TMI recommended that the trainings include the broadest possible mixture of managers. The goal was to get people from different departments to know each other better. The only exception made was to separate out the ship captains, many of whom had limited English skills.

Breaking Down Silos

After the programs, one of the comments heard repeatedly was how much everyone enjoyed getting to know each other. When crew members are on a ship, they do not have much interaction with crews from other ships in the line. But because of vacation schedules, department heads were rotated to other ships in the region. Ultimately, many of them would work together. When that happened, they would not be entirely unfamiliar with each other.

Combining people from all parts of the business added a new dimension to the program. Participants shared stories and examples and stimulated each other with ideas. They loved partnering with people from other departments to do experiential exercises. This helped create new relationships that would never have formed if the programs had been organized department by department.

As the sessions progressed, TMI facilitators observed managers from different departments sitting together in the dining room. Before the mixed programs, crew members would take their meals with people they knew or who had the same job functions. After they had gone through the program's exercises, they had more to talk about than time permitted in the sessions. This resulted in extended discussions after the sessions and created opportunities for ship leaders to sit down with people they might otherwise have missed.

For newly hired people, being able to form relationships with experienced managers was invaluable. They felt the support that was offered as they began their new careers with this company. They talked about feeling part of an extended family. People spoke about what a great experience it was working together and getting to know everyone.

Comments like this reflect what happens when people learn together and work through different viewpoints that they naturally bring from their own departments. Each department saw its particular mission as central to the company's operations. For example, managers of shore-side excursions believed they had to take care of the guests all day long, while hotel managers only had to feed guests and ensure their rooms were in order by bedtime. Hotel managers would respond, "Try running a cruise ship if there are no staterooms." Food-and-beverage managers would defend their role by saying, "Try getting people to come on cruises if the food isn't outstanding." When these people were brought together, they learned more intimately what each team did and what its challenges were—and why all of them were essential. They actually offered new and different ways to help one another do a better job for their guests.

Transformation in truly excellent operations will likely be relatively small. Moving guest satisfaction ratings that run in the high nineties to numbers closer to the one hundredth percentile is not easy. Service approaches do not have to be completely rewritten to transform the guest experience. Sometimes a small change, such as in how people are grouped together in training programs, can have a major impact on how service is actually delivered.

Transformational Questions

1. How can you build strong relationships and mutual understanding between your teams? What impact would this have?

2. What issues do your guests complain about that might be best addressed if your staff members had better relationships with each other?

3. What could you change about your service offering that does not focus on what you teach your team but rather on how you structure that learning?

4. What assumptions do you make about what your staff needs to learn to get better at service? Do you assume that new service techniques always have to be learned?

CHAPTER 9

Of Service and Crêpes

Alice Kaboth and Carolin Reiter, Consultants, and Bernward Mönch, CEO, TMI Germany

Customer service transformations in large, complex organizations present different types of challenges. By adopting a fresh, experiential methodology, with consistent messaging over a period of years, tangible organizational change can happen. It requires a partnership between the external consultants and the most senior members of the organization. Without that collaboration and support, this type of transformation is unlikely to happen.

"If we want to become the most highly regarded service company, we have to begin with our executives. We can't just focus on the people who work directly with the customer. We need everyone to help." So said the CEO of a German telecommunication company.

The telecom leaders wanted their employees to learn a new German approach to delivering service. Germany has been known as a "service desert" for many years; as the saying goes, "Good service in Germany is about as rare as rain in the Sahara." The leaders wanted change that they understood could not be achieved through a bottom-up method that would only reach employees who were in direct contact with customers.

The executive board wanted a change in the organization's total service culture. Board members put it this way: Service orientation was to become an essential element of the company's culture. If leaders were aligned about the importance of service, it would impact everyone, touching all departments, sectors, and management levels. This was no small undertaking as the executive level consisted of more than two thousand employees. The board needed help.

TMI Germany was asked to design and facilitate a Service Academy, compulsory for all executives. This academy was conceptualized not as a physical location but as a mental space. It would provide space for sharing, learning, and contemplation. The executives needed to question their own work and attitudes: What do I think about service behavior? What role does service play in my work? How can I, as an individual, affect the success of our company by looking at service?

> *Service orientation was to become an essential element of the company's culture. If leaders were aligned about the importance of service, it would impact everyone.*

First Steps

The telecom's journey began in 2008 with several large kickoff events. To put the participants in the right mood for the coming changes, the events were situated in upscale locations. These events were not exclusively focused on service delivery. The goal was also to enable the participants to personally receive excellent service themselves.

Coffee breaks were used to display extraordinary service. They became memorable affairs. Sumptuous repasts with crêpes, coffee, and fruit were arranged. But instead of being served by the off-site staff, the executives put on aprons and gloves and made the crêpes, chopped the fruit, and brewed the coffee themselves. They had to, in short, provide service for each other, pleasing and serving their colleagues as they promised their customers in marketing messages. Every break they swapped roles. First they received service. Then they delivered it. Their task was to deliver the best service quality possible. They outdid themselves—and each other!

Today a picture in the entrance area of the TMI offices in Munich speaks of the Service Academy's beginnings. It shows the current CEO of this telecom company in a red apron, tossing a crêpe. He has a big smile on his face.

Following the kickoff year, three-day reality training programs were held as part of the second year of the Service Academy. A Frankfurt consultancy organization was hired to design a fake company, which the participants would work with during their training. Participants would either hate this experience or love it. It was a risky concept. The thought was that by looking at another company's approach to service, the telecom executives could actually look at themselves without getting defensive.

After classic but exciting concepts around internal service were delivered on the first day, the participants received details about the next day during dinner: "Starting tomorrow, you will work with a company for two days. Currently, the company is experiencing economic difficulties. You will work there as task forces for two days. Among other things, you will focus on the company's service issues."

To make the whole situation believable, the executives were taken by bus to the fake company's location. A bus driver decked out in full uniform greeted them. When they arrived at the building, the participants could see the company's flags and logos, and they met a number of employees. The made-up company's CEO (an actor) welcomed and thanked the telecom executives for their helping.

During those two days, small teams of no more than six people had a coach who was with them throughout the day. The coach provided detailed feedback after each event. This setting allowed observation of the participants' behavior in real situations. Nobody could say, "This is just a workshop situation. In real life I would have reacted differently."

Of course, the participants had their doubts. Many assumed that this organization could not be a real company, as nobody had ever heard of it before. This is the modern Internet era, and the participants whipped out their mobile phones and laptops and began to look for that company online. This was anticipated, so the participants were able to find the company's website, an online shop, the address, and contact details. Everything was there as if it were a real company.

The coaches were not deterred by questions and doubts. Some of the participants asked, "Excuse me, but is this actually real?" The coaches responded, "I don't understand the question. What do you mean by that?" Some participants tried to push the envelope about the company's existence. One of them asked, "This company does have a branch in the United States, doesn't it? I'd like to call someone there now."

Without any excitement at all, as if this were a question asked all the time, the coaches told the executive that they would look up the American colleague's direct cell number as, given the time zone differences, it was still early in the morning in the United States. The people in our fake company's central office (disguised as the Accounting Department) frantically searched for someone in the United States they could call.

One of the coaches knew someone who currently was in the United States and could play this role. He was called and briefed for the part he would play, saying, "Someone is going to call you in a few minutes. Answer the phone, 'This is David. How can I help you?' Tell the caller you're from the company he is currently advising and answer his questions. Just get involved with it, improvise." The call went well. The executive's questions were answered and he hung up satisfied that he was working with an existing company.

The participants had never experienced learning like this. They got feedback from the coaches that awakened them from their executive sleep. Even today, a lot of them say, "Those were the two most intense days I've ever experienced in my life as a manager." Seven years after this workshop, telecom managers are still impressed by the insights they gained—and use in their everyday working lives.

The first year's phase consisted of the large kickoff events. The second phase involved the practical, three-day workshop around the fake company. In the third phase, the executives had direct contact with their own customers. These three elements formed a perfect mix of fun, exciting challenges, and a serious approach to a serious topic.

After the first three phases, the executives asked for an annual, compulsory, two-day workshop. These workshops became a fixed component of their working lives for several years. Almost every one of the two-thousand-member executive team looked forward to them. The challenge was to make these follow-up workshops as exciting as the first ones. Ultimately, the executives were offered interesting interactive programs, each with a different format.

For example, the topic of service quality was combined with the topic of leadership. The link was made to show that great customer service also means being service oriented as a leader or manager. After all, customers can be other employees inside the organization.

The topic of service quality was combined with the topic of leadership. The link was made to show that great customer service also means being service oriented as a leader or manager.

An art college was engaged to help produce an art module. Among other exercises, the executives were asked to draw one picture of "service"—as a team. The challenge of this task was that the participants were not allowed to talk to each other while they were drawing. The principle that was being followed was "Learning begins when you leave your accustomed ways of behavior." This exercise was difficult and frustrating for many of the participants.

Most exciting was to witness how strong emotions and behaviors, such as rigidity and anger and joy and helpfulness, were displayed during the art experience, although no one said a word. The coaches turned these experiences into deep learning for the participants.

Also introduced was a game called "Friday Night at the Emergency Room," which is designed to reveal how people are able to work together as a team in crisis situations. As the exercise proceeded, it was easy to see who thought of the patients—or their fellow medical staff—as customers. When discussing the game afterward, the teams realized that they did not "waste" time thinking about which strategies to use—especially in an emergency. They simply started acting, without asking themselves if their choices made sense. Most of the participants later confessed that this was their behavior in real life. If they had to put in place any of the executive board's new decisions, for example, they started implementing without considering what they were doing.

In another of the annual workshops, actors were employed. One of the actors played the role of Napoleon Bonaparte. He had just returned from his battle at Waterloo and was now talking about himself as a leader. Another actor was a flight attendant who talked about service quality in her job. Several other actors slipped into different leadership situation roles.

All these situations had one focus: service and leadership. Seeing and hearing the actors talk about these topics gave food for thought to our executive participants. The participants thought about themselves as human beings and as contributors to the telecom company. They stopped looking at themselves as people who simply filled telecom positions.

Because coaching was available throughout every part of the learning exercises, the executives got feedback on their behavior in specific situations. This is a luxury seldom provided for workshops that touch this many participants. Remember, the target group included two thousand people. In the end, this constant coaching may have been the element that made the Service Academy the transformational success it became.

TMI Germany also enjoyed the unconditional support of the telecom company's executive board. Every single one of the board members backed the transformation processes. To emphasize the importance of the learning experiences, the executive board members themselves attended the events once a year. They expected the same behavior from the two thousand leaders. The executive board members' regular attendance at evening events and their willingness to talk to the company's top management team led to a special relationship among the executives.

> *Every single one of the board members backed the transformation processes. To emphasize the importance of the learning experiences, the executive board members themselves attended the events once a year.*

At the completion of every module, the managers could book a Service Academy for their department's team members. For those most directly involved with service to customers, service quality modules were created and offered. As a result, learning continued through the huge organization.

What Changed?

Telecommunications is a tough and highly competitive industry. Customers are ready to go to Yelp and complain about everything. They treat telecom companies almost as if they were utilities. So the goal of becoming the most highly regarded service company in Germany was not an easy one to reach. Even though things changed inside this giant telecom company, the consultants will be the first to admit that they could not measure the academy's success as concretely as they would have liked. However, the executive board saw changes that were considered proof of the initiative's impact.

During kickoff events, observers could see how the initial distance between the participants turned into collaboration and joy when colleagues networked with each other. People who were thrown together and did not know each other became a unified team of executives. After the second event, participants stopped bad-mouthing or making fun of their company. Everyone took his or her work seriously. Everyone knew, "Yes, we are good. Yes, we can be even better."

The mind-set of the telecom executives changed, which enabled them to be aligned on the important topic of service. Every leader—no matter what his or her management level—took responsibility for the service quality of the whole company. All of them began to assume personal responsibility for the behaviors of their call center employees and even the vendors in their retail shops. These behaviors showed up in their performance reviews of their employees and the increasing number of personal visits to call centers and retail shops.

> The mind-set of the telecom executives changed, which enabled them to be aligned on the important topic of service. Every leader took responsibility for the service quality of the whole company.

In this company, people came to realize that everybody has an influence on service. In a drastic exhibition of commitment to this principle, executives who refused to accept this proposition were made redundant. The Service Academy also shaped awareness that there were not only external customers but also internal customers. Service quality at the telecom company meant improving service to internal customers as well, so even a controller can influence service quality for customers—for example, by improving customer interfaces and speeding up administrative processes. Alignment about these changed mind-sets could be seen.

Things Change

When the human resources director, who basically ran the Service Academy inside the company, resigned, the director's replacement changed the focus of the company. The new HR director decided that after several intense years, the time had come to use company resources for other projects. The last event took place in a huge medieval castle surrounded by a large park and forests. The main house is protected by its original moat and has been in the hands of one family for over two hundred years. It was a worthy location for an end to such an era.

Is transformational learning possible? TMI Germany has no doubt of that. The telecom's executive team had walked its talk for several years. Again and again, people approached TMI consultants with incisive feedback as this giant company made changes itself. They could all spot differences in the executive team as its members transformed and grew.

Transformational Questions

1. How do you get all leaders and managers in your organization to take ownership of the transformation process so that change is not seen to be the Change Department's or HR Department's responsibility?

2. Are you taking risks on new approaches or remaining on the beaten track in your organizational transformation approaches? A famous proverb says, "If you aren't living on the edge, you are taking up too much space." What does that proverb mean to your corporate learning approach?

3. The stakes are most often high in terms of the benefits of change and the consequences of not changing. How can you commit your board or senior team to invest resources over an extended period to achieve the desired change?

Aligning Customer Service across Multiple Borders

Ariel Jasovich, Director, TMI Argentina

Every company wants to build stronger relationships with its customers. An important first step is to work from the inside out. Get your leadership and your people to align so teams working together with stronger relationships will support your goals.

As it is in many parts of the world, the Latin American chemical industry is highly competitive. Many multinational chemical companies offer great products and innovative service. They all employ aggressive pricing strategies. Remaining a leader in the Latin American market requires constant focus for all the players in the field. Above all, the companies that lead in this industry must have the ability and desire to adapt to customer needs. Unless they want to compete solely on price, they also need to provide quality service that differentiates them from their competitors.

The subject of this story is one of the leading chemical companies in Latin America. With business units including Food and Pharmaceutical, Animal Feed, Industrial, and Pigments and Sulfates, it is a serious company with serious customers. It has large operations in Argentina, Brazil, Colombia, and Peru. It also had recently acquired many smaller companies within its four countries of operation.

The company advertises itself as being in the solutions business— solutions for its customers. It sees science as filled with surprises. As it says, "New chemical compounds are created as atoms join together to solve problems and create new products." The company uses this metaphor to talk about how its talented staff surprises its customers and adds value to client businesses. Working together with clients across national boundaries, this company has a mission to create an interconnected network of excellence for its customers.

The problem was that the business had lost its edge. The company was a good company, but its broad geographical area of operation and all the recent mergers and acquisitions had left staff confused. Processes were often ineffective, and strategies were poorly defined. Customer service was less than excellent.

So the president and his executive team proposed a new approach to building stronger customer relationships: focus on the client. They named the program "Customer Intimacy." It included improving technology, internal processes, and human performance to provide better service than currently offered.

The challenge for TMI Argentina was aligning over six hundred leaders and employees from different countries, departments, and organizational cultures. Aligned language, attitudes, and approaches were essential. After lengthy discussions with company leaders, a highly customized Putting People First (PPF) program was chosen to be the vehicle to communicate and reinforce the company's service values. These values would be the nucleus for the project, aiming for a cross-border alignment in both behaviors and attitudes.

Furthermore, a decision was made to approach the challenge from two directions. On one side, the company leaders would be supported to make sure they knew how to encourage, communicate, and implement the full scope of the change. On the other side, the company would identify service level agreements (SLAs). SLAs are normally used to describe the standard of service to be delivered to external customers and typically cover items such as response time, quality, and service recovery. However, this company used SLAs to describe how service was to be delivered internally—to colleagues, other departments, and its locations in the four countries in which it operates. Ultimately, the internal SLAs would impact how external customers would receive service. Many SLAs required reinforcing and fixing procedural weaknesses that were present because of the company's cross-border operations and because of the lack of alignment resulting from the numerous mergers and acquisitions.

Consider the mood at the beginning of the project. Both leaders and employees suffered from a lack of motivation and communication, poor integration between geographic locations, and misalignment of service objectives. Everyone was aware of the challenges and had few positive expectations about the probable results. This was understandable given the scope of the company's operation.

But all employees put their hearts and brains into the task at hand once the PPF programs began. The PPF programs were offered to both blue- and white-collar employees. And it was in these collaborative workshops that more than 40 percent of the SLAs were produced.

Hundreds of people worked together with their teammates. They had serious fun identifying what was and what was not possible to offer to the company's customers. As a result of this approach to setting standards, staff members saw themselves becoming part of the change that was occurring around them. This was a genuine surprise to them. They had expected orders from their bosses to make the Customer Intimacy transformation happen.

> *Hundreds of people worked together with their teammates. . . . Staff members saw themselves becoming part of the change that was occurring around them.*

Getting all employees involved in setting their own service standards gave everyone ownership of the change initiative. The company's leaders saw that their teams could be inspired to help with the corporate initiative. Getting employees to take responsibility for providing the best service to customers would not be left up to just the leadership team.

But to accomplish their goals, the leaders had to engage with their staff to help and support them. The leaders insisted that they were already doing this. However, it turned out that they were not, and they quickly learned that because they attended the PPF programs right along with their staff. Open feedback was forthcoming in these meetings, which was critical for alignment.

Employees began to describe their change behaviors as "bricks." Each changed behavior or brick was added to the new structure they were building. They spoke with pride about what they were creating together, brick by brick.

Together, the members of the chemical manufacturer's staff were able to identify dozens of ways to lose their customers. They learned that it is not difficult to "fire" customers. But they also found dozens of ways to improve their service results. More than that, they found they were part of an organization that wanted to change.

Attitudes also began to shift within the company across the entire region. After all, participants in all locations were getting the same Customer Intimacy messages. They were also working on the same processes and SLAs.

By this point, TMI had inspired a clear *why*. Now the challenge was *how* to make it happen at a concrete day-to-day level. After the SLAs were stipulated, TMI set up a service clinic, in which leaders learned how to operationalize their new status quo. No one wanted the company leaders to say, "This isn't the way we're used to doing things." While that was a true statement, it could not become an excuse for not making changes.

The *how* part of the transformation process was hard because of its complexity. Yet hard does not mean impossible. Company leaders learned how to set up precisely defined SLAs that were measurable. Not only were the SLAs uniform, but they could also be tracked the same way regardless of the country.

Customers from each of the four countries would know what they could expect across the region. It would not matter if they were in Argentina, Brazil, Colombia, or Peru. Accomplishing this uniformity was not easy because the differences between these countries are considerable, including language differences. Portuguese is spoken in Brazil, while Spanish is spoken elsewhere. The political and economic differences among these countries are also significant. So unifying an aligned approach to customers took some time, and it meant everyone from four different cultures had to be on board.

Why did this initiative work across this broad region? Three things happened that proved critical:

- Similar values, behaviors, and standards that were customer focused unified the company across the four countries of operation. These clearly defined values also enabled the company's recent acquisitions to work from the same page. The company wanted a consistent level of service offered everywhere, and this meant coming up with a clear picture of what this would look like.

- Involving both leaders and staff in the process meant everyone got to take part in meeting the challenges. Putting everyone in the same programs created opportunities for staff members to talk with each other across departmental lines and up and down the command hierarchy.

- Working with the leaders in service clinics meant company employees were supported in figuring out how to implement the defined SLAs in their local operations. They were assisted every step of the way.

Transformational Questions

1. If you know the *why* of the changes you are aiming for, do you also know *how* to make them happen?

2. What would be the reaction if you mixed your communication experiences so people from different levels of the organization were present at every meeting addressing your proposed change?

3. How do you involve your employees in your change process? If you want them to own the process, how can you get them involved?

4. Are you looking at alignment among your leadership team, between leaders and the rest of your people, and across different operations within your organization? What is your plan for alignment?

CHAPTER 11

When Old Meets New

Ayşegül Drahşan, General Manager, TMI Turkey

Generation Y employees can spark a change in leadership style if everyone else travels with them. When capable leaders, employees, and suppliers live according to a set of shared values and act like one team, enormous success can follow.

This story is about a 100 percent Turkish concern traditional in its management approach and surviving over sixty years of economic and political turmoil. Dedicated to the principle of giving back to society, this thriving business has approximately twenty-four hundred employees. Its business activities are concentrated in five integrated areas dealing with the automotive industry. Over the last ten years, it has achieved an average annual growth of 15 percent despite the economic crisis that began in 2008. Most people in Turkey recognize it as a shining example of how far the Turkish economy has advanced.

TMI Turkey's entry into the story began with a telephone call from the company and a brief explanation of the problem. The revered company had become aware that its traditional style of management needed to change so it could attract and keep younger, Generation Y business school graduates.

The company had just appointed forty-eight Gen Y newcomers (hereafter referred to as the Group of 48) to managerial positions. The Group of 48 was tasked with driving the business into the future. All forty-eight members came from different holding companies, and they all had different backgrounds.

This group would work in the headquarters of the company in Izmir. The ancient city of Izmir is small compared to Istanbul, but still it is a bustling city of almost three million. It has a recorded urban history of over four thousand years and is surrounded by a half dozen other ancient cities. It is the major port for Turkish exports, and because of a booming economy, a growing number of young Turkish professionals live there.

Every single member of the Group of 48 was a sophisticated young professional. It was clear from the beginning that they needed a program unique to them. The company wanted to create a leadership team for the future, different from the existing leaders who had grown up with the company.

After an initial meeting with a varied group of managers, a needs analysis was planned that would provide input for a customized transformation leadership program.

It was clear from the beginning that they needed a program unique to them. The company wanted to create a leadership team for the future, different from the existing leaders who had grown up with the company.

The corporate human resources director and the Group of 48 joined the meeting, at which TMI consultants described the needs analysis they would conduct. The director emphasized that these forty-eight professionals were to carry the rest of the company and its employees into the future, which needed to be tied to the company's values. The company's HR managers and TMI Turkey would cocreate a training program to develop a more modern style of managerial competency. TMI was also asked to create an approach that would internalize the company's values throughout the rest of the company, as well as among the company's dealers and suppliers.

After many meetings, fieldwork, 360-degree appraisals, managerial team workshops, and the needs analysis, a two-year manager development program was agreed upon. The program had the full support of the corporate Human Resources Department. The preimplementation analysis and investigatory activities had provided the necessary creative space to develop a customized program that met the company's needs.

The Program Launch

A kickoff meeting with stakeholders (corporate leaders, company heads, and HR directors) was recommended for the company. The Group of 48 was the star of this meeting. The members were up to speed about what was happening as they had participated in the initial investigation process. During the kickoff meeting, all stakeholders received a clear road map about the two-year program, complete with project aims and targeted outputs. Members of the Group of 48 were given descriptions of positions they would soon hold.

One point of anxiety was apparent. The kickoff meeting included one-on-one sessions with the company's president. Members of the Group of 48 were apprehensive about the appraisals they would have to go through. However, when they felt the strong support they were receiving from the whole company, they understood that the program had been set up to ensure their success. Some said later, "Whew! I thought it was going to be more like business school—competitive, with a bunch of us getting failing grades. I can see now they really want all of us to succeed."

TMI Turkey's Role

The entire development program was evaluated session by session so TMI could track the progress of the program. Because the company's leaders were eager to experience the impact of this special group, TMI facilitators created a sense of urgency. The members of the Group of 48 began to see that the future was already around them and that their job was to make sure they got there without wasting time.

The new leaders were challenged with reading materials, articles, and homework. They joked that this was no different from their time at the university. They also received one-on-one coaching that focused on how they implemented their learning action plans. The good news was that all the participants came through the two-year program with flying colors. The next step was to plan a graduation ceremony.

Graduation as a Reinforcing Step in the Project

The graduation ceremony was a memorable event that is still talked about. It lasted three days! The members of the Group of 48 took the stage one by one. They answered questions from the senior leaders in the organization. Some joked that it was like a beauty pageant.

The questions included

- What would you change if you had more authority than you currently have?
- What do you see yourself doing five years from now?
- What immediate changes will you apply to your department?

The answers were funny, significant, and moving, and the leaders in the organization could see their future standing on the stage. Delight was on the faces of the management team. They had been kept informed every step of the way about what was happening, and now they could see the results.

Moving the Implanted Values to the Next Level

The second phase was to impart the organizational values to the next level of employees, so work was begun on a program that had to be as good as or better than the original project.

The company's values were simple: We are respectful. We add value. We continuously improve. We are result driven. These values are easy to depict on wall posters that people often stop noticing immediately. So the challenge was (and continues to be) to imbue these values with life in the organization.

> *The company's values were simple. . . . The challenge was (and continues to be) to imbue these values with life in the organization.*

The TMI team quickly saw from watching employees talking about the values that the heart of each simple statement had to do with communication, inspiration, and sharing. With this in mind, a half-day workshop was created, filled with activities based on singing, drawing, and acting. The groups attending were large—up to eighty people in each workshop.

All workshop activities reflected the company's values. For example, managers did not *tell* staff about the values and how to live them. Instead, the workshop participants described what the values meant to them and how they affected their work. One could observe that the values were becoming internalized. The process of internalization reflected the change in management style the company was instituting.

There was some anxiety expressed about employees singing, acting, and drawing. But when the executives saw the release of energy and the creativity of these large groups of employees, they were sold. Original songs that came out of the workshops now play in the company factories. Televisions at the entrance of the headquarters building show the performance sketches that were created and acted out in the workshops. Now, everyone who enters the company's buildings—employees, customers, suppliers, and visitors—is treated to these enactments of the company values.

This was a new experience in the organization's history. Artwork, music, and theatre could bring values to life and make them easier to remember. This was not child's play. This serious implementation reflected a different style of learning and engagement. Everyone could see it.

TMI Turkey also worked with the company's dealers and suppliers. Special workshops were organized where the dealers built robots that represented what the company's values meant to them. They showed them off at the end of the program. This was the first time dealers and suppliers had a program set up just for them. As a result, barriers dissolved, and now their relationships with the company are stronger than ever.

The company's ultimate goal was to create togetherness among all the managers, employees, suppliers, and dealers. It wanted to show everyone involved with the company how to live a set of shared values and act like one team, which is exactly what happened.

Two years ago, this company was a thriving business. Today it is even more successful. The employees are committed and continue to do what is necessary to reach their targets. So what changed?

There is a qualitative difference in how the employees work. Now they work not only with their muscles and brains but also with their hearts. The feeling of belongingness is palpable. People who work there call themselves "a family." The future leaders of the company, all from Gen Y, are as committed to this company as previous leaders were. They do not have to look elsewhere to find opportunities to grow. They see that their future is in this remarkable company.

Transformational Questions

1. What types of activities might bring home your values so people really accept them and start living them?

2. Are you attempting to teach transformative approaches with standard classroom techniques? Could there be a better way? Should you consider different ways of involving your teams?

3. Do specific groups within your organization need transforming that could kick-start a much larger transformation project?

CHAPTER 12

A Russian Bear Takes on Complaint Handling

Jeffrey Mishlove, COO, TMI US

Transformation at huge organizations can be elaborate, sometimes running several years before significant change is seen. On other occasions, by focusing on a single idea, change can be quick. This is especially true if the CEO is willing to put his or her name behind the idea.

This transformation story is about a large Russian company. Sometimes all TMI can do is sit in awe on the sidelines and watch a company transform itself around a single idea.

This company is a bank with over a quarter of a million employees and close to twenty thousand branches spread over Russia's eleven time zones. The size and scope of this operation is breathtaking.

A New Approach to Service

How do you get a single behavioral idea into an organization of this size? When a new president came to the bank, his first message to employees was that the bank had to change dramatically and that the first step was to "to turn the bank's face toward customers." It was not that easy to do given the size and history of the company. The bank reached out to Nadezhda Bogdanova, who was the head of TMI in Russia. Her team developed a special program on service with the slogan "Everything Starts with Me" that introduced the TMI concept of A Complaint Is a Gift. This conceptual way to look at complaints is also a technique that customer-facing staff can readily adopt. A decision was made to use the Complaint as a Gift concept as a way of doing business at the bank.

The Process

The scope of introducing this idea was enormous. With the support of TMI Russia, here is how the work was done and supported.

The bank took a public position on customer complaints. News releases with the vice president's name attached stated that the bank was adopting the philosophy of A Complaint Is a Gift. The releases, issued both in English and Russian, said that the bank believed that effective complaint handling is the cheapest and most effective way of improving the bank's business. It was a message both to the public and to the bank's service staff and managers.

Briefings by the bank's corporate officers were made to the regional managers so there was little doubt that the message was coming from the very top of the organization.

The bank's leaders were not nervous about staking out a public position in this area. At one evening dinner, Janelle Barlow, coauthor of *A Complaint Is a Gift,* delivered the keynote, speaking to invited guests who were the heads of most of the biggest organizations in Russia. The bank wanted some of its major customers to know that it was going to do everything it could to retain customers, particularly when they had problems. "It's not," as a senior bank officer said, "that we like complaints. No one does. But we still want to hear them so we can learn from them and turn our relationships with nervous customers into solid relationships."

Large-scale messaging campaigns were undertaken. Janelle Barlow was invited to Moscow for a series of presentations and high-level meetings. One meeting in Moscow with over a thousand people in the audience was simulcast to bank branches throughout Russia. Some thirty thousand people watched the presentation in real time. The video was subsequently put in the bank's library and used as part of an ongoing educational program.

The bank's president sent a communication piece to the bank's managers about *A Complaint Is a Gift*, telling them "This is the book I want you to read." To get a buy-in from everyone reporting to them, they were told that corporate training programs would be available on the subject. The president also said he would tell all the bank's partners to read the book so they could let him know if the message was working. The book was, in short, required reading for everyone from managers to operation workers. A popular book in Russian was published about the bank; in the book the concept of A Complaint Is a Gift is described as a "cult." The author made it a point to ask employees at every branch he visited whether they had read the book. The bank's leadership was clear: if the book was not read, then the idea could not be applied. The author found many employees who had learned to listen attentively to the bank's customers when they complained.

The bank set up a large lending library through its Corporate University. The top three books on the list were *The 7 Habits of Highly Effective People* (Stephen Covey), *Good to Great* (Jim Collins), and *A Complaint Is a Gift* (Janelle Barlow and Claus Møller). An order was placed for twenty-nine thousand specially printed copies of *A Complaint Is a Gift*, translated into Russian, with a foreword by the bank's president. The books were distributed and placed in the corporate libraries set up around the country.

Was the book a cult? No, unless *cult* means devotion to a business idea. If this is the case, then TMI would say, "Go ahead and take it to that level." We know that it is difficult to get simple ideas like A Complaint Is a Gift institutionalized in small teams. So to make it happen inside a giant corporation like this bank in such a short time frame is quite remarkable.

> *Was the book a cult? No, unless cult means devotion to a business idea. If this is the case, then TMI would say, "Go ahead and take it to that level."*

It definitely requires the support and backing of a charismatic leader, which this bank has. If you know a prominent person from outside your organization who can bring significance to the idea, then enlist his or her help as well.

Transformational Questions

1. Is there a single idea you would like to stand behind that can be integrated into your organization fairly quickly and easily? If so, what is that idea?

2. What is the best and most efficient way for you to communicate a single standout idea?

3. What will you need to do to promote the idea beyond lending your support? What structures and resources in your organization already exist that can build on the support the idea is given?

PART III

Shifting Mind-Sets to Transform Cultures

H enry Ford, the great carmaker, is reputed to have said, "Whether you believe you can do a thing or not, you are probably right." That statement is the heart of cultural mind-sets. If a group of people who work together can be convinced that a transformation is possible, then a first step has been taken to change.

Organizational culture consists of the values, beliefs, and behaviors that drive how things are done. If you want to transform a culture, you have to create shifts in mind-sets. These shifts need to happen at senior levels of the organization, followed by changes in behaviors. Without senior-level champions for the new thinking, sustainable transformation is not possible. The shifts in mind-sets need to cascade down through managers and to customer-facing and non-customer-facing employees.

As will be seen in this part, simple questions can start the process of senior-level mind-set shifts. Concerted efforts by senior management can create excitement around new ways of thinking. With persistence and energy, simple ideas can shift the mind-sets of large groups of employees.

CHAPTER 13

The Heartbeat of a Culture

Edward Matti, Managing Partner, TMI Middle East

The quality of a transformation depends on the quality of the questions that are asked at the beginning of the project. These questions might seem simple, yet they helped an organization address important and even sensitive issues by provoking both thought and action.

Established in the early 1970s, TMI Middle East's client, an automotive group, has gained a reputation for quality, integrity, and trust. Both customers and suppliers alike commend its service quality and operational style. It has twenty-two branch locations and enjoys approximately a quarter of a billion dollars in turnover.

As with many other developing and profitable companies, challenges are always present. The group has a team of 714 staff dispersed over 310,000 square kilometers. As a result, it struggles with developing its core business proposition through such a widespread business structure.

The group's leaders knew they had overlooked one of the most important aspects of sustaining a successful enterprise: a strong organizational culture. They began to look for new ways to increase levels of employee engagement and customer service. They wanted a solid culture that would differentiate their business from competitors, reasoning this would, in turn, further drive performance and profitability.

TMI met with the group's senior management team to discuss the matter. TMI had been dealing with this automotive group for some time on other projects. So this project was a continuation of a solid existing relationship.

There was a sense of excitement in the room at the first meeting. The group's leaders were happy they were finally tackling this issue. They had confidence that TMI could design a solution. They naively thought that TMI would simply tell staff what to do and teach them how to do it. It did not work out that way.

Well into the meeting, TMI consultants asked two short but complicated questions: "What is your current culture? And what do you wish it to be?"

The room fell silent. Some people attempted to answer the questions but could not come up with a clear response. At this moment everyone realized how deep the challenge was. To get to the desired culture, a transformation initiative was needed. It was not going to be just a "training program."

The leadership team became anxious. They were high performers, and they wanted to be able to answer these questions definitively. So the general manager assembled a team that would assist TMI with getting the answers. Supposedly, Marketing, HR, and other departments would define the culture of the group, and then TMI would teach everyone how to relate to it. Again, it did not quite work out that way.

The Emancipation of a Culture's Heartbeat

TMI set out to better understand both the people who worked for the group and the environment in which they worked. All the employees could describe their roles in the group. For the most part, everyone was delivering the required results. They knew there must be more, but they were not quite sure what it was.

Using the Five I's approach (investigation, identification, implementation, integration, and inspiration), TMI was able to identify a powerful three-step solution. This solution, which took nine months to put in place, assumed that the group's successful culture transformation had to focus on both its environment and on staff behaviors. A value proposition was created with the following objectives in mind:

- Service—How does the group get everyone to speak the same customer service language? How are staff engaged and inspired to provide exceptional service (once exceptional service is defined)?
- Teamwork—How can the group compensate for its lack of professional and relational skills in the organization? How does the group get everyone to think as one team, with one heart?
- Behavior—Where do we start? What defines our behaviors, and how can we make those behaviors sustainable?

Aha Moments

One pleasure in working on initiatives of this type is watching a client experience an "aha moment." This often happens when our clients pour their hearts and souls into the goal of positive change. An aha moment means the client has taken a leap.

One such aha moment came after several lengthy meetings during which a long-term culture transformation strategy was hammered out. Somebody said, "A cultural heartbeat." At that moment, the general manager's face was filled with delight and excitement, much the same as when a child opens a beautifully wrapped present. It was as if every part of him was tingling with the awareness that this approach would indeed make the group stand out from the competition. At the same time, it would bring them together as one culture. Cultural Heartbeat became the name of the initiative.

Together, the group and TMI cocreated an experience and a future they would both feel proud of. Intense discussions preceded every step along the way. The first part of the journey was built around three culture change modules. They would be communicated in both English and Arabic to 131 customer-facing staff. The focus was on the after-sales team.

The coaching sessions gave everyone an opportunity to put his or her new understanding into action as people shared best practice ideas with their colleagues.

Besides the culture change modules, TMI consultants coached the team leading the initiative inside the group. The coaching sessions gave everyone an opportunity to put his or her new understanding into action as people shared best practice ideas with their colleagues. Most important, recognition went to the customer-facing staff for their efforts.

Business Rituals: The Way Forward to a Stronger Heartbeat

Set practices, called "business rituals," were created to focus on follow-up. What are rituals in a transformation process of this type? They are activities that support the changes after new ways of working are introduced. Everyone wanted to make sure the after-sales team lived the newly defined values. This meant the team members had to exercise their beliefs every day, be it at the office or at home.

A dedicated e-mail address and phone lines were set up. Using these communication tools, the team members provided the feedback regarding business rituals they were practicing. TMI recorded the events and collated the data on a weekly basis. At the end of each month, TMI selected three Cultural Heartbeat winners based on their involvement, their interaction with internal and external customers, and the frequency of their engagement. The group's senior management team recognized Heartbeat winners with trophies and certificates during an awards ceremony.

By the end of the first year of using the business rituals, the group had recognized twenty-seven Cultural Heartbeat winners. Several were fast-tracked into more senior positions.

A support framework was also set up within the group to provide clear communication to every member. This ensured that the Cultural Heartbeat would resonate loudly within the entire group. Thirteen communication channels, published in both English and Arabic, were created.

The Never-Ending Throb of a Heartbeat

The group's employees currently practice almost four hundred business rituals. These rituals define the exceptional personalized service now offered to customers and colleagues. The practice of these rituals has brought about positive interactions within the group across the entire country. Employee engagement, business performance, profitability, and customer service levels are still on the rise.

Moments of truth, those moments when customers evaluate the service they are receiving, are now tracked. Lifetime memories from these moments of truth have been embedded in the group.

Since the launch and application of the Cultural Heartbeat initiative, the general manager of the organization has been promoted to group general manager. His efforts on this initiative were a key factor in this well-deserved promotion.

> *Moments of truth, those moments when customers evaluate the service they are receiving, are now tracked. Lifetime memories from these moments of truth have been embedded in the group.*

Here is how the general manager summarized the impact of the cultural transformation project:

> With the support of TMI Middle East, the commitment of our senior management team, and the utilization of the cultural change support framework, which ensures a consistent tone and delivery of internal communications, I believe that the "Heartbeat" within our business will continue to develop until such time as it will not only be heard clearly by every member of our own team but also resonate loudly with our customers and be a defining way of providing differentiation in a very competitive business segment.

And all this started with two simple questions: "What is your current culture? And what do you wish it to be?"

Transformational Questions

1. What is your current culture, and is it what you wish it to be?

2. While you may use training as a tool for culture change, have you defined the process that will reinforce specific behaviors that define your culture?

3. What loud, visible communication devices do you use to make sure everyone knows what is happening in your organization?

4. What rewards and recognitions are in place that everyone can see and celebrate?

5. Are people getting promoted because of your organizational transformation? How could you do this?

6. Have you defined business rituals? How do you support and track them?

Racing toward a New Reality: From Sports Car to Formula One Racing Car

Anna-Maria Pepin, Managing Director, TMI Switzerland

How do you awaken your organization if it has fallen into the success trap—a mind-set of complacency? It is not easy, especially if it is a giant. Awakening can hurt, and it takes a lot of time and persistence. But it can be done, as this story demonstrates.

In dynamic, competitive markets, a certain state of mind can lead to decline. This state of mind easily happens when your reach is global, consumers love your products, and you are highly successful. Without constant mental and emotional adjustments, people inside successful organizations are virtually guaranteed to develop this mind-set.

This type of complacency occurs when companies believe they are invincible and have no need for change. This seems to happen more frequently when the company is a giant. But as we all know, even powerful giants can take a tumble. And because of their size, they require a lot of help getting back onto their feet.

This is the story of a giant that did stumble. But it did not fall. The company, one of the world's biggest brands, was global. It was profitable. It was a model for FMCG (fast-moving consumer goods) companies.

Business analysts in the company started to detect early warning signals. These signals projected dangerous trendlines that indicated the company was falling behind in manufacturing, operations, and product distribution. The handwriting was on the wall, and by the early 2000s, the chairman and group CEO recognized that it was time for a change.

Trying to Awaken the Giant

The board hired a new CEO. His goal was to shake up what became known within the company as CCT—complacent culture thinking. The board members charged the new CEO with business transformation and used a racing car metaphor to explain what they wanted. The mandate for the new CEO was to convert the giant into a winning Formula One racing vehicle. The car would become sleeker and faster. It was an apt, solid metaphor.

The new CEO made changes. Restructuring occurred, new strategies were introduced, and job cuts were made. And with this came confusion. Employees who had been loyal to the company for years became stressed. They watched their long-term colleagues being cast out from the organization. Morale plummeted. Confusion reigned.

Not surprisingly, the CEO was replaced. You could already hear the pit crews—the company's loyal employees—saying at the announcement of a new CEO, "Here we go again—another CEO, more changes, more job cuts, more stress."

A Different Approach

The next new CEO realized that the organization, above all, suffered from a mind-set problem. Employees across the company were not engaged. Productivity was down. Employees were frustrated and felt the company had lost direction, which was a new experience for them. This CEO felt the need to reignite a sense of trust and pride. The first step was to create a new vision and to focus on a set of values. The CEO aimed for both a top-down and bottom-up approach. He established clear operational priorities and goals that

> *This CEO felt the need to reignite a sense of trust and pride. The first step was to create a new vision and to focus on a set of values.*

everyone would understand and then put in place. In doing so, he wanted to establish a sense of direction to engage employees.

The CEO knew that he could not do it alone. He needed his cultural architects—the people reporting directly to him who would guide the change implementation. Beyond his team, he needed specialized expertise.

TMI Switzerland was given the responsibility of providing assistance to achieve the desired transformation, alignment, focus, motivation, and high-performance engineering. It was a big order!

The CEO was aware of the hills that needed to be climbed. He knew that there would be resistance to change. He knew that his pit crews around the world were still disbelievers. Who could blame them after they had endured several years of what they thought were disastrous efforts at change? After all, previous changes had resulted in serious tumbles. Why would or should they believe the CEO? As they said, "Here we go again: change, change, and change just for the sake of it. We can't take any more of this."

What TMI observed within the company, in addition to disengaged staff, was a high level of inertia and complacency, as well as a crucial lack of open, honest discussions and feedback. Communication was based more on top-down commanding than on empowering people.

Lengthy talks between corporate leadership and TMI led to a conclusion: the company needed to move from a traditional hierarchical structure to a more networked organizational structure. Only in this way could the company be successful in the new and changing business world. The decision was also made that the change would be limited initially to the Swiss operation.

Such a change would dissolve the traditional command-and-control structure and replace it with a genuine culture of empowerment. It also entailed a change from being task oriented to being result oriented.

Employees had been brought up in an environment of command and control. They knew nothing else. In this new world the pit crews heard the words *empowerment, ownership, trust, feedback, coaching*—yet no one knew what they really meant for day-to-day operations.

Those fuzzy management buzzwords needed to be linked to results. As a targeted response to this need, the CEO championed an overarching principle: "Zero Waste—One Team—100% Engagement." When put in concrete terms, this principle could inspire the pit crews to believe in the process and become winners.

This formula was highly ambitious, so it had to become the focal point for everyone in the organization. How could the CEO win over the heads, hearts, and hands of the pit crew to ensure lasting change? This goal could be achieved only if all crew members had a clear understanding of where they currently were—at a very dangerous turning point with low productivity, low staff morale, low quality, and low client satisfaction. They also had to understand the direction in which they were headed. And they needed to be given the means to win the race.

> This goal could be achieved only if all crew members had a clear understanding of where they currently were. . . . They also had to understand the direction in which they were headed. And they needed to be given the means to win the race.

Perhaps most important of all, the pit crews had to see, hear, and feel the messages of the journey from the very top. This meant that the members of the senior team—the cultural architects—had to believe, too. They were role models, even though they had previously been seen as part of the problem.

The level of urgency for successful change was high by the time TMI joined the project. This project had to succeed. Otherwise, the employees in the Swiss division would lose the last bit of trust they still had in their company.

TMI Switzerland, together with the CEO and the cultural architects, created a series of ambitious goals, including the design and delivery of strategies, events, training programs, coaching, feedback, and experiential and accelerated learning. This multifaceted approach would touch the whole organization in a number of different ways.

The pilot kickoff was a major event known as GPGP—Great People, Great Performance—opened by the CEO. Once the GPGP was approved, this project then cascaded top-down from senior to middle managers, each time with the presence of the CEO or one of his cultural architects.

The mantra, "Zero Waste—One Team—100% Engagement," repeated again and again, was used to fill up fuel tanks to get to the goal of total team engagement. The aim was to fuel the whole organization with the new vision, strategy, core values, and right behaviors, followed by sharing and celebrating success. Complementary strategies were built into the infrastructure in the form of learning programs focusing on caring, resourcefulness, safety, health, and environmental sustainability.

The GPGP intervention filled both the client and the TMI team with a great sense of pride. Why? Because, it worked emotionally. People left the GPGP sessions feeling reengaged and ready to lead their pit crews with a strong sense of belonging, empowerment, and trust. They wanted to take action. This was fuel for their passion.

Behaviors started to change after a few GPGP sessions, combined with road shows driven by the CEO. Company values were being lived, not merely preached. This became more and more apparent in everyday conversations across all the Swiss pit crews. A change in the language could be noticed within the organization at management levels—from "do what I tell you" to a positive language of empowerment. This change was supported by the development of a feedback, coaching, and continuous-improvement culture.

Within four years, the transformation had moved down to pit crews: team leaders and individual contributors. The pit crews felt that a faster car was achievable. Confident in this belief, they developed personal action plans to help move the change forward.

The CEO was delighted with the success. As he put it in a public testimonial in June 2015, "TMI's attitudes are contagious—and if attitudes are contagious, then TMI is worth catching." Today, the way teams win is understood by all. The transformation toward the end goal of "Zero Waste—One Team—100% Engagement" is being lived and observed through everyday successes, coupled with a shared sense of belonging.

Why It Worked

You might ask how and why this process worked in such a gigantic operation. First, and most important, pit crews became aligned with the giant's strategic direction. They did this because of the way they were brought into the transformational process. They felt respected and believed they were an important part of the turnaround of the Swiss operation.

Second, the GPGP sessions created a shared understanding. Employees at all levels left these experiences understanding the importance of the corporate vision and values and being aligned with the strategy, business principles, and priorities. The vision started at the global level and connected the departments with a common purpose.

Third, excitement was released in the GPGP experience. This excitement was used both to write personal action plans and to remain focused on them.

As an engagement and alignment of both hearts and minds occurred, the giant lost its mind-set of complacency.

Transformational Questions

1. How do you deal with the mind-set, created by past failed transformation efforts, that "this is just another fad; it won't happen."

2. What is the consequence if people do not grasp that true transformation involves many changes until the best formula emerges?

3. When people want to structurally change your organization, how can you help them understand that they must first engage the hearts of the people who will implement the change?

4. How can you make sure your communication efforts actually touch people's emotions and fuel their energy?

CHAPTER 15

The Power of a Smile

Janelle Barlow, President, TMI US

Smiles can be contagious. Read how the smile became a call to action for defining a service culture. The results were outrageous and sensational!

Everyone who teaches customer service addresses the topic of smiling when interacting with customers. It is an idea that has been around for a long time. In fact, a very old Chinese aphorism is "A man who does not smile should not open a store." Good advice.

Getting staff to understand the power of smiles is *not* a challenge for service companies. They already know that. However, something gets in between what they know will work and their ability to actually put those smiles on their employees' faces. Another challenge for service providers is to keep their smiles going when feeling exhausted after a long day, or upset by bad news from home or by a difficult interaction with a customer or a supervisor, or stressed out after too many days on the job prior to a deserved break.

> *Getting staff to understand the power of smiles is not a challenge for service companies. They already know that. However, something gets in between what they know will work and their ability to actually put those smiles on their employees' faces.*

An even bigger barrier to freely given and authentically felt smiles is a management culture that tries to get staff to smile by simply telling them to do that. "Now you smile when you are in front of a customer" is a barked command shouted at staff too many times. Years of bad habits and bad thinking inside a service company can quickly stop or mute the best smiles. The practice of hiring people just to fill positions means anyone will do—even people who really do not like to smile. After all, the reasoning goes, how difficult is it to say hello to and smile at the customers when they walk in the door?

You can easily see whether the culture supports a positive customer service attitude immediately upon walking into any establishment where personnel are there to greet and help you. This includes the entire hospitality industry, retail banking, department stores, healthcare, and the cruising industry. You can tell what is going on in a corporate culture within seconds by looking at the faces of the employees.

If employees do not smile, perhaps the management team has gotten into the habit of issuing orders to their constantly changing customer-facing staff—managing by fear. Maybe they shout at their staff behind the scenes. Perhaps systems in the company do not support staff development or encourage high levels of motivation. Perhaps the organization consists of segregated departments that discourage cooperation across organizational silos. Maybe wages are too low or people are kept on a part-time basis so health benefits do not have to be paid.

Creating a New Service Culture

So when TMI US was given the opportunity to work with a newly formed cruise company that had just launched a new prototype ship with an entirely new crew and a new brand, TMI leaped at it—a fresh start with a soon-to-be-formed service culture. At that time, the ship itself was only a skeletal structure and no crew was on salary.

About one-third of the eventual crew had had experience on other cruise lines. The other two-thirds were new to cruising, new to the cruise company, and new to this ship. Of course, everyone was new to the ship. This included both front-line crew members who would interact with customers and everyone dealing directly with taking care of the ship or handling other ship operations, such as the laundry, kitchen, or engine room.

In our initial visits with the company, the TMI team spent time with the most senior people on the ship—a highly experienced team in charge of making sure that the ship was ready to go by a certain date. Staterooms had been booked. Advance deposits were already in the company's bank account, and the sailing deadline had to be met. The TMI project met the Human Resources team and had a hard time believing how carefully they were recruiting new staff—no "warm bodies" for this team, in spite of the time pressures on them.

Once the senior team understood TMI's plan for how to create a customer-focused service culture, they gave TMI the green light—and a lot of trust. TMI's team joined with another outside consultant to the project. This consultant was highly experienced in the cruise industry, and perhaps best of all, he knew of TMI's work. He even had attended a Complaint Is a Gift seminar years ago, after which he immediately tested one of the key service-recovery tools with a complaining customer. From then on, he was a convert to the way TMI taught service ideas. One of the cruise line's senior project managers had attended a Time Manager seminar years prior and knew about TMI's style of engagement and ability to create transformative behavioral change in short periods of time. The members of the cruise line's senior team were committed to "inviting" people to leave the organization if they did not fit the proposed high-energy, customer-focused, and smiling culture. The TMI design team had their support.

While the ship was being built and travel arrangements were being made for crew members to arrive five months later, the process was begun of developing an entire service culture curriculum and designing an actual tool kit for the soon-to-be management team.

The process started with a leadership program that had one important message. The success of the maiden voyage and all other cruises that followed was dependent on how the managers interacted with and supported their crew. The crew, if supported, could do the heavy lifting and were capable of creating amazing experiences for the guests. The managers were reminded that if the crew were not happy and smiling, then it would be difficult to get happiness reflected from the guests.

The cruising industry is highly competitive, and the customer base targeted by this cruise line is one that just about every high-end cruise line seeks—seniors around the age of sixty-five who have the resources, sophistication, and time to travel. Millions of these people live in the United States alone. Americans in particular not only want a great cruising experience but also want friendly, smiling crew members who will quickly fix any problems they encounter. And for this, they will tip generously.

Understanding the considerable effort and cost required, TMI still recommended a full two-day service experience program for *everyone*, including the senior team. Everyone needed to hear the same messages and to be invited into the same culture that was dubbed a "we" culture. Everyone understood that this was a unique and, indeed, historical cruising event. All crew members understood that their responsibility was not just to the first ship and its first guests. The crew on this first ship would set the tone and pattern for the entire line as more ships are built in the years to come.

How Did TMI Get the Crew to Integrate the Idea That Smiling Matters?

Transformation typically does not happen in classrooms if ideas are taught in the traditional way of "Here's what you need to do. Now go out and do it." That lesson might last a few days, but people quickly revert to ingrained behaviors.

TMI facilitators had to build a culture around the response to a smile, making it more likely that guests would feel a special connection with the crew. The crew had to embrace the message in the famous song from the Broadway musical *Annie*, that "You're Never Fully Dressed without a Smile." While the crew knew that tips would be larger if they created an amazing service experience for guests, they didn't know that they themselves would be less likely or more likely to be in the mood to smile based on the culture in which they worked.

Program facilitators set about building team spirit inside the class-room. All the program leaders talked about a "we" team and developed exercises for the crew to experience what this meant in reality. Games were played and everyone was rewarded with candy, praise, and applause. The large groups laughed a lot, sang songs, and watched some very unusual videos that illustrated the service points. TMI trainers brought incredible energy to the groups of sixty in each session. They loved these very special people from all over the world, and in return the crew loved the facilitators.

All the while TMI snapped pictures of the crew members smiling. Slide shows were made of just their faces so they could see what they looked like with big smiles on their faces. Incidentally, they looked beautiful. Probably nothing is more confident and attractive than a fresh young face with a big smile.

This was their first experience with the cruise line they had made a commitment to, and they were blown away. Comments were heard such as "My gosh, if this is what the training experience is like, imagine what it's going to be like on this first-of-its-kind brand-new ship." Materials were created so each team member was able to personalize a fold-out card that fit inside his or her nametag holder with the ideas that stood out the most for that person. At the end of each two-day service experience program, four groups of approximately 240 people were brought out into a large foyer to form two large, facing circles. They were asked to share their personalized cards with the person opposite them and then move on to the next person. It was a din, a celebration of a group of strangers who came together after two days, unified in their approach to best representing this cruise line. It was, in a word, magical.

Several TMI facilitators involved in the project were invited on the "shakedown cruise." They lived with the crew on the ship for another seven days. They took more pictures of them, now smartly outfitted in their uniforms and always with huge smiles on their faces. Everyone watched them jump in and solve several major prob-

> They listened to guests talk about the service they were receiving. Some described it as "a miracle." They could not believe how confident this neophyte crew looked and behaved.

lems. TMI listened to guests talk about the service they were receiving. Some described it as "a miracle." They could not believe how confident this neophyte crew looked and behaved. The experienced cruisers on this initial voyage knew the industry and understood how difficult that first cruise can be. They were in awe of how in control, friendly, and always smiling the crew were.

This experience was a transformative one for the crew. Many told TMI representatives that. The people with previous experience had never fully realized the power and impact of their smiling interactions with guests, which included using their names and looking at them directly. Those crew who had no experience in the industry, who had little experience with any formal work, and who were fresh out of school also understood what a special opportunity they had been given on their first job.

The TMI team also experienced the power of smiling in a much more profound way than ever before. Smiling is such a bedrock in the service experience that it is easy to ignore its importance. In fact, many people downplay the power of smiling in service. But when you make it the linchpin of what you are offering guests, all of a sudden the guests feel what it's like to be surrounded by people who are happy at work—as witnessed by their smiles. They feel as if they are being hugged and appreciated wherever they go. Service is no longer transferred from one person to another but rather a shared experience of joy and energy.

This is a perfect environment for a cruise! And it is a transformative experience for both guests and service providers.

Transformational Questions

1. What does your service operation understand about the power of a smile?

2. Do your managers and supervisors talk about smiling as something to do, or do they work to create an environment where people naturally want to smile?

3. What is going on in your culture that makes people who experience it want to smile?

4. If your culture is years or even decades old and it is not a smiling culture, what will you have to do to change it?

5. If you see inauthentic smiles, what might this tell you about your culture?

6. Do your managers and supervisors smile, or is the expectation of smiling just for people who are customer facing? How can you convince managers their smiles are as important as those on customer-facing employees?

Exploring Is More Fun Than Attacking

János Balázs Kiss, Managing Partner, TMI Hungary

Sometimes an analogy can be the perfect mechanism to shift thinking about what needs to happen to start a transformational process. Such was the case with this Hungarian pharmaceutical company.

I t was the end of a training program, and the last participants were leaving. The head of TMI Hungary, János Balázs Kiss, was shutting down his computer and packing his last pieces of equipment. Reaching for his phone on the table, he noticed an incoming call. He did not recognize the number, but when he answered the call he did know the voice. It was Tibor.

A couple of months earlier, Tibor attended a program facilitated by TMI Hungary for a major Hungarian pharmaceutical company. The subject area was emotional intelligence. Tibor was a researcher with a broad range of interests. He spent the evenings of the first and second days of the program with the TMI consultant, talking about life, work, and what it meant to discover new drugs. It was like being at a TED presentation with Tibor talking about the latest developments in chemistry. The conversations were stimulating and definitely memorable—especially for the consultant, who had studied history at university.

A Request for Help

"I need your help," Tibor said on the phone. "I got promoted. You are talking to the new head of original research."

The two men had talked about this possibility. Tibor wanted that position as it would give him a platform to explore new ways of looking at drug research.

Tibor continued, talking fast. "I know exactly what I want to do, but I need a team that can work together. They need to get to know each other. I'm taking them on a retreat where I want them to turn into a team, and I want TMI to help."

A couple of days later, the two acquaintances met in the building where the company was then housed. The company was moving into a brand-new high-tech site in two months. Tibor was excited. He was a newly appointed leader with new ideas. He was given an opportunity to introduce change in the way he and his team worked together. And his team would have a new, top-of-the-line working environment.

Researchers as Explorers

Tibor talked about his metaphor for drug discovery: "Most people doing research in pharma think about it as a fight. The language we use reflects it: we defeat illnesses; we fight to extend life; we talk about altering the malfunctioning of proteins; we combat diseases; we find a spot to attack; we identify targets," he explained.

The consultant interjected: "Outside pharmaceutical research, military language is used in the same way. In companies there are missions and strategies, headquarters and the field, the sales force and front-line staff. This language also shows up in personal development. There's a recently published book with this kind of language in the title."

"Exactly!" Tibor responded. "I think there is a better approach to life and development than fighting. I think a better and more suitable paradigm is exploration!"

Tibor was passionate. "A researcher's or scientist's primary motivation is curiosity. Think about geographical discoveries. People explore because they have to know what is out there! And if there is a high mountain, we need to climb it. Remember that old saying 'Why do people climb Mount Everest? Because it's there.'"

As any effective consultant will do, the head of TMI Hungary summarized, "So you think that the best paradigm for chemical research is mountaineering?"

"Precisely!" Tibor paused for a moment as if to let that sink in. He then continued, "Different fields of therapy could be thought of as mountains. Different peaks stand for the pathologic indications. The scientific approaches based on specific mechanisms are the routes to the peak. For example, one therapeutic area is the central nervous system. It's the mountain range. The different pathological indications include schizophrenia, depression, and mania. These are the peaks that need to be conquered."

Again, he hesitated to give the consultant time to ingest what he was saying. Tibor knew he was not a scientist. "If we think of schizophrenia as a mountain peak, for example, the different faces of the mountain are equivalent to a variety of pharmacotherapy approaches. These approaches are the biological mechanisms that various neurotransmitters affect. The suspected path mechanisms, such as dopaminergic, serotonergic, and glutamatergic mechanisms, are where routes fork, run parallel to each other, cross each other, and reach the peak in different ways. They depend on the type of dopamine, serotonin, and glutamate receptor group or subgroup. The point is that there are many ways to climb that peak. But they need to be explored."

Not fully comprehending everything Tibor was saying, the TMI consultant nonetheless got the gist.

The scientist continued: "Our research expeditions are made by groups consisting of highly skilled—and preferably experienced—researchers. They set out from base camp, which is the place where teams get ready. They make all the necessary preparations from there. Base camp is also the place where the support and service units are based. These units carry out structural, analytical, physicochemical, and molecular biological functions. Objectives are set for the trek. Information is gathered that tells us the route we choose will indeed take us to the peak. Then we start to climb."

Tibor's use of this metaphor did feel more exciting than fighting a battle.

He went on: "The processes that serve as our chemical starting point are established at base camp. The biophysical and biochemical screenings, which in climbers' terms give information about the best places to build base camps higher up on the mountain, are also carried out at this place. Management is located in the first base camp. This means that management sets the objectives of the expedition—one of our research projects, that is. Management allocates the necessary resources and budget and considers how much risk is involved with the proposed project.

"The interesting thing," Tibor noted, "is that although management assumes this responsibility for the whole project, it never leaves base camp, never joins any of the research teams. Oh, and it also monitors the progress of the various teams just like in mountaineering. The people on the mountain have to have clear communication with the people staying at base camp. Base camp managers monitor and assess risk and provide support so the climbers can stay focused on exploring."

The consultant liked the analogy. He said, "Still, you can climb Everest in many different ways. What's your preference? Are you planning to use oxygen, for example?"

"That's the point. You can do it like Sir Edmund Hillary, or you can choose the Reinhold Messner way. I'd prefer the second. Messner, the alpinist from South Tyrol, was the first who did it clean, without supplementary oxygen. He used fewer porters and resources. In comparison to Hillary, who literally attacked the mountain, Messner explored it."

It was easy to see how relevant this was to the reality of the company and Tibor's vision for the Original Research Division. And probably even more important, Tibor's passion was strong.

Sometimes consultants need to energize people or give insights. There was no need for these here, except for one insight that could help Tibor understand how this all tied into the retreat they were discussing.

"If you're talking about exploration as an analogy for drug discovery," the consultant suggested, "what if we use the analogy for the retreat itself? We can start there. How about if we invite your key people to a journey of discovery, to an expedition?"

So far the two had not talked about changing the mental mind-set of the newly assembled team. What Tibor originally had in mind was a two-day team-building retreat. Yes, he wanted his team to be informed about a new approach. But mostly he started out wanting a team-building retreat so everyone could get to know each other better. Now a new approach was beginning to take shape.

"I see," Tibor said. He was a quick learner. "You're talking about involving them in this metaphor. You're saying let's invite the leadership team to the base camp to plan our future exploratory expeditions together."

This was exactly what the consultant had in mind. He recommended showing the team what Tibor meant by his approach. The team members would experience the Messner way together. They would work on creating a culture where this approach was built into it right from the start in the first team retreat.

Getting Everyone Involved

This is where the cultural change process started for this pharmaceutical company. It began by involving the leadership team and the researchers. Everyone who would be at the retreat provided input. The process of sharing information about the vision began as the two-day retreat was designed.

Because of the passionate vision of the new head of the Original Research Division and the involvement of other stakeholders in the company, the "Base Camp retreat," as it was called, created the necessary cohesion in the culture right at the beginning. And this is the best and easiest time to shape a culture.

> Because of the passionate vision of the new head of the Original Research Division and the involvement of other stakeholders in the company, the Base Camp retreat created the necessary cohesion in the culture right at the beginning. And this is the best and easiest time to shape a culture.

Everyone at the Base Camp retreat took part in the refinement of the vision. When you build something, you start to take responsibility for it. The group named their approach Origo. The name reflected the original research they would conduct. It also meant a new starting point from which they would set out on their exploratory journey together. The metaphor of mountaineering meant they would give themselves space to explore a mountaintop. They would not attack it. And they would operate as a team with support organized at their base camp.

Did this group scale mountains? Developing new, safe drugs that work is a lengthy multiyear process. Project Origo has been ongoing for over two years, and TMI Hungary has been with the group every step of the way. The researchers are not just attacking a specific illness. They are exploring alternate climbing routes as they proceed up their mountains. And they are finding that this is a powerful position from which to conduct original research.

Tibor's team is currently attempting to scale their first peak. The very sophisticated scientists on the team have been energized by looking up, seeing the mountaintop, and figuring out how to get there. At the same time, they are exploring some interesting alternative routes. The team is making the journey together. Original research that considers health needs and devises solutions for these needs is very much a start-and-stop process. But with the mountaintop kept in view, the researchers can see where they are going even while they explore.

The Origo team has been reminded of the story that is told about NASA, the group that landed the first persons on the moon on July 20, 1969. Remember, NASA worked for almost ten years to land Neil Armstrong and Buzz Aldrin on the moon and bring them safely back to earth. The NASA scientists and engineers experienced a lot of failures along the way; they explored a lot of false paths until they got it right. Some of those false paths resulted in new discoveries.

The metaphor of climbing, as opposed to battling or attacking, has led to a complete shift in how members of the unit work together.

One of the NASA engineers was asked how he kept his focus for all the years he worked on the project.

He replied, "It was easy. Whenever we got discouraged, we would just go outdoors and look up. We could see our target waiting for us."

Exploring new routes to a mountaintop that is clearly visible has motivated and unified the Origo team. The metaphor of climbing, as opposed to battling or attacking, has led to a complete shift in how members of the unit work together. Their focus has been intense, and the team remains motivated.

Sometimes a relatively simple shift in how people view their work can create a culture that is vibrant and team focused.

Transformational Questions

1. What is the metaphor you use to get your teams to work together? Have you thought through your metaphor to determine the impact it will have on how you and your teams work?

2. What values are contained in the metaphors you use that reflect the desired culture of your organization?

3. What well-known historical figures reflect how you want to approach your work? Can they help you clarify your transformational process?

CHAPTER 17

It's Not Easy, but Cultures Can Learn to Soar Again

Veronica Fernandez, Head of Consultancy, TMI Spain

This transformation story is set in the period of the global economic meltdown that began in 2008 and has continued until the present time. The company's culture was negative and consumed by fear about poor financial performance. The company was able to shift its focus from poor performance to people, previous strengths, and positivity. In the process, it succeeded.

TMI Spain's client was an airport business services company mired in operational problems. It faced an economic crisis at the same time. Part of the economic mess was outside its control. Powerful economic forces impacted the world—in particular, the Eurozone. Company leaders were so focused on ending a cash hemorrhage that many failed to look at their people.

Initial conversations with this client revealed two contradictory attitudes. People either felt deceived and burned out or felt eager to improve and put the crisis behind them. No one was sitting on the fence about the company's future.

TMI Spain's journey with this business group had originally started back in the 1980s. A two-day Putting People First program was presented at that time for members of the Airline Division. The PPF program focused on employees as individuals. At that time, it was a huge vitamin shot in the arm of this company. Because of the program's engagingly presented messages, the company experienced a revitalization of energy that resulted in enhanced passenger experiences. This, in turn, resulted in a dramatic increase in passenger travel and positive feedback. Both passengers and employees loved the company.

A transformation had occurred, and it worked. But time passed, and the economic crisis that began in 2008 took all the oxygen out of these positive intentions, which were, after all, some thirty years old. Vitality from the original approach was diminished in the midst of real and huge economic challenges.

> *A transformation had occurred, and it worked. But time passed, and the economic crisis that began in 2008 took all the oxygen out of these positive intentions, which were, after all, some thirty years old.*

In 2010, TMI had also worked with the Aircraft Maintenance Business Unit. In that division, middle managers supported the proposed path of change that placed an emphasis on leadership development. At the end of 2013, the Airport Services Division asked for a repeat of TMI's people engagement and management leadership efforts. The Airport Services Division wanted to replicate the success of the original program. However, the situation was not the same as the one that TMI faced in the 1980s and in 2010.

TMI's first step was to get a clear picture of the new situation. What had changed? The economy of 2013 was strikingly different from that of the 1980s. Yes, the Airport Services Division was part of the same business group, but the world had changed dramatically. The airline and airport service industries themselves were not the same; budget demands had changed things. The Airport Services Division could no longer survive with only one airline client; it had to work with other airlines.

While all this was going on, Aena Aeropuertos, SA, the state-owned company that manages airports, was opening the bidding process to find a supplier to offer airport services at Spanish airports. Getting ready for the bid was a huge undertaking. Middle management in the Airport Services Division was not aligned with the strategy of its airline clients. This lack of alignment threatened Aena Aeropuertos' choice for the Airport Services Division to handle the millions of bags, passengers, and thousands of aircraft that went through the airport every year.

Lord of the Rings

Six thousand employees staffed the Airport Services Division. Its various departments were not unified. Employees had even come up with shorthand language to describe the different groups at the airport, using characters from *The Lord of the Rings* to describe their attitudes. As nearly as TMI could tell, this labeling was an attempt to understand what was happening at the airport. No one was offended by these designations. But anyone who has seen *The Lord of the Rings* movies knows that fighting is a strong component of the story line, and infighting reflected the reality of what was happening at the airport.

Elves were the airplane logistics staff. Everyone knew they liked their work; they even approved of the recent restructuring that occurred at the airport. Nevertheless, fear about the future was contagious, and they were afraid of losing their jobs. Unemployment in Spain had rocketed to new heights.

Customer services employees were dubbed as Middle Earth humans. They took care of all processes that involved contact with passengers. They had a strong customer focus, but they had defined that focus in their own way, and it was not necessarily aligned with other trends going on in Middle Earth. Most of them had been in their jobs for over fifteen years and were reluctant to change. Many of them exhibited burnout.

Operations employees were the orcs. They provided aircraft handling services. There were more orcs than any of the other characters. The orcs did not have high levels of formal education, but they had a strong and unified team feeling; they were ready for change.

Everyone seemed to agree that middle managers were not interested in change. They did not feel they belonged to any of *The Lord of the Rings* groups. They also did not feel they had the support of senior management. They said they had no idea what was expected of them. It was clear that this company needed a profound operational and cultural revitalization.

TMI has learned over the years that the easiest time to create a successful business culture is when the operation is new. Then the needs of the organization can be aligned with behaviors and standards that are set at the same time. The most difficult time to change a culture is when the patterns are entrenched and people's behaviors no longer work to reinforce the organization's success. However, a crisis that has everyone shaken can also help speed up transformation. Both the country and the Airport Services Division were in the middle of just such a crisis.

Many employees in the company had inherited an attitude that said, "Take care of our customers, and we will be okay." It had been reinforced over the decades but was in danger of being destroyed because of internal fighting.

The company was still benefiting from the customer-focused culture that had been established some thirty years ago in its Airline Division. That was something upon which to build.

Many employees in the company had inherited an attitude that said, "Take care of our customers, and we will be okay." It had been reinforced over the decades but was in danger of being destroyed because of internal fighting. Clearly attitudes had to be changed and aligned.

The Challenge

Given the complexity of the situation, the TMI team conducted an investigation to gain a more complete understanding of airport operations. The team also assessed the feelings and attitudes of those enabling planes to take off and land safely. Success happened when planes flew, fully loaded, with contented passengers who had their luggage secure in the plane's baggage holding area.

One key issue was that management was unaware of the many concerns of people who worked at the airport. The managers knew employees were discouraged and frustrated with the economic crisis. They did not know that their own behavior was also seen as erratic, untrustworthy, and part of the problem.

Nonetheless, the managers expressed love for their company. The sense of belonging was as high as any TMI had seen in Spain, especially during the years of the economic crisis. People said that they felt the current situation was like a lover's betrayal. Feelings were strong and ranged from pain and disappointment, to fear about the loss of their safety nets, and to curiosity about what new change was flying into the airport.

Airports are beehives of activity. Some times of the day had heavy workloads. At other times people did not have a lot to do. Most operational positions had different types of contracts: fixed regular, fixed irregular, and temporary. Each had its own privileges and drawbacks. Over the years, these differences created a strong feeling of unfairness.

Communication from management was not clear. Insecurity occurred when the organization failed to explain decisions, policies, guidelines, and actions. As a result, an intense distrust of leadership threatened the project to transform the company's culture to something more workable.

Word leaked that the group directors got substantial pay raises and the former CEO received a huge golden parachute when he left the company. At the same time, general staff salaries were reduced by 11 percent, reportedly because of poor productivity. People had no idea what they should believe. But they felt the system was unfair. The unions attempted to communicate with employees—at all levels. They took a protective attitude toward staff. Still, employees were not happy with the union's actions and believed its influence was largely negative.

People were also suffering from a lack of recognition or feedback for positive behavior. Managerial feedback tools were based only on correction and reproach. To defend themselves, managers said they felt their hands were tied. They did not feel that they had the power to change wrong or nonproductive behaviors. Nor did they feel they could reward excellent behavior. In addition, the vast majority of managers were accustomed to a hierarchical leadership style. Most were about to retire and had little desire to try anything new.

Remarkably, the people in charge of customer service felt that they did not have responsibility for day-to-day issues. The managers kept their thumbs on the supervisors who reported to them. The supervisors felt they needed to address poor performance only when situations became serious. When faced with a serious issue, they pushed it up to their managers. The supervisors, rather than working to solve problems, spent their time on administrative details. It was not a pretty picture.

On the positive side, in spite of the heavy weight on his shoulders, the Airport Services Division director was supportive of the transformation project. He took the project on as his own and made the most of it. Also, the new generation of employees was eager to change. These employees had fresh energy, got involved with issues at the airports, and wanted to know what was going on. It was their future and they wanted to be in charge of it.

Success Arrives

TMI Spain brought together the people who were strong supporters of the project. They were to become its internal backbone. In exchange for their support, they demanded and received continuous feedback and a high degree of transparency.

Part of the challenge for the TMI team was that they heard multiple versions of the truth concerning many situations. The steering team and TMI finally began to accept that there were, in fact, multiple realities. This required multiple approaches to address each situation. TMI and its internal supporters had to avoid becoming discouraged by the negative attitudes held by many employees.

Nevertheless, the Airport Services Division director encouraged an approach that pulled out all the stops. The first step TMI took was to create a series of short-term communication strategies. TMI and the director met with the unions to presell the project. Their engagement and support was essential. The airport director began holding informal meetings with small groups of managers to improve internal communication. These meetings no doubt saved the project. The director was able to set appropriate expectations for what would happen, and the managers' initial reticence broke.

The steering committee defined organizational action plans to respond to the most urgent needs. These included increasing communication, introducing a new style for how leaders approached their teams, modeling the recognition of good work, and having managers step up to the plate to actually get involved in operational issues when people suffered from overload.

TMI earned the support of unions and managers. People who took part in the professional development program were intensely involved. The organizational action plans were implemented gently but with firm steps. Confidence was being gained slowly and steadily.

Rekindling pride in one's work was necessary. A collection of success stories helped with this objective. The shared stories generated a lively and healthy competition among departments. The language people used started to change. As one aircraft ramp services worker told us, "The jargon here has changed. We've gone from negative to positive. New things are in the air."

In the words of TMI's client, this project was the "trigger and inspiration" for change. It catalyzed the process of transformation toward a culture of excellence, reinforcing unity and collective commitment. Earnings before interest and taxes went from −21 percent to +4 percent in 2015. The director estimated 15 percent of that improvement was related to increased productivity and cultural and attitude change. And the company won the bid from Aena!

Here are several reasons why this project worked:

- The project was built on the bones of a culture that had already transformed itself once. Many of the desired attributes were still in place and became the foundation for positive change years later when a new crisis presented itself.

- Cultural transformation projects require finding what is right and is working and then building on those strengths. The organization also had to find what was wrong. But this process was set up to learn how to focus on building positive change. For this project, strength was found in a single strong and committed individual in the division.

- Sometimes emotions are so strong that it seems people can focus only on the negative, pointing fingers at who is to blame. Middle managers are handy scapegoats in situations like this. The same is true of unions. In this case, however, the temptation to blame was resisted. As a result, middle managers and the unions became champions for transformation.

- To transform an organization facing overwhelming issues, you have to focus on the champions. They are people in the business who will add life to the project. They, like airline elite fliers, are the ones who need special and specific attention. In this case, the champions were the new generation of employees.

It was time to replicate the project in other airports in Spain.

Transformational Questions

1. What are the strengths of your existing culture that can help build new mind-sets in you transformed culture?
2. Who are the champions you can work with to support the changes you want to make?
3. Are any groups in your organization being blamed for current problems? How can you work with them rather than buy into the dominant meme?
4. How do you deal with problems that need fixing so you can focus more on what needs strengthening?

CHAPTER 18

From Good to Great

Rossitsa Hristeva, Deputy Executive Director, TMI Bulgaria

Business leaders were challenged by the ideas in the widely read book Good to Great *by Jim Collins. While it is one thing to be challenged by ideas, it is another to attempt to implement them. This transformation story is about a company that did just that. It was not an easy process nor a short one. But the results have been remarkable.*

This story is about a large, international electric company with operations in Bulgaria. It enjoys a sustainable operation, solid business development, and a solid market share. For more than seven years it has been rated as one of the best employers in Bulgaria. Its sales team has in-depth experience. People on this team are knowledgeable and professional. They are offered new approaches to sales and management in the form of regular training programs.

You may be wondering why this company was ripe for a transformation. In spite of its success, troubling indicators were visible.

The effects of the world economic crisis on this company were tangible. Fewer customer orders resulted in a reduction of factory employees. Key performance indicators measuring employee engagement were dropping. The new market was hostile and more demanding. The company needed to be flexible and to differentiate itself from its competitors. While the company was still the undoubted leader in its field, to preserve this position, the leaders in the company decided they needed to go from "good to great" in line with the best-selling business book by Jim Collins.[1]

By 2012, well into the economic crisis, the new human resources manager in Bulgaria decided that something needed transforming. The sales team had grown up with the company. They did not lack for self-esteem given their past sales records. Still, some old-school thinking was appearing, with people talking nostalgically about the "good old times." They were not used to having competitors breathing down their necks. To outrun them would require more effort than they had displayed in many years.

This is a company that believed in people. Senior managers were convinced that great people make great organizations. Top managers naturally concluded that they needed to grow their sales leaders to a new, more mature level. If they had an integrated approach to leadership in the region, they would be able to operate consistently. Good to great was possible.

A New Hope

The moment was exactly right for the president of the operations in Bulgaria, Albania, Macedonia, and Kosovo to come to Bulgaria. He was energetic, devoted, and open to listening. He also wanted to take the company to a new level. *Hope* became the buzzword for a new level of capabilities and motivation and ultimately the company's continued successful growth. This client did not need a training and development program. It had been using this approach for years. It wanted a trusted consulting partner who could help it achieve practical, sound results and transformation of the leadership team. The top team was clear: the mind-set about leadership needed transforming.

This transformation required a consulting team that not only had the right approach and global know-how but also had capability to work throughout the Balkans—Bulgaria, Serbia, Slovenia, Croatia, Bosnia and Herzegovina, and Montenegro. TMI was asked to present to the electric company's leadership team.

Two TMI consultants, Vesselka Tsocheva from Bulgaria and Olga Svoboda from Serbia, had worked together for over ten years, establishing and developing a strong consulting presence in the region. They shared the same passion and belief about what good leadership and people management mean for business growth.

A small meeting was arranged in Belgrade for the consultants to introduce themselves to the company's leaders. Vesselka and Olga entered with authenticity and a great deal of spirit. They demonstrated they were on the same page with their ideas of leadership transformation. They even finished each other's sentences. The client's HR manager and HR zone managers saw them as a living example of how strong leadership could boost their own company.

The Way

TMI was selected to create an approach that would transform this company from good to great—as Vesselka and Olga heard on more than one occasion. A standard leadership development program would be inadequate. This client required an accelerated transformation. Something different needed to happen. The electric company's leaders wanted to see an immediate outcome in the real world. They wanted to see people changed because of their investment. Rational, unemotional content would not create this growth acceleration.

Only an impact on values, emotions, and the mind-set of the managers would accomplish the desired difference. Emotions drive behavior,

> *A standard leadership development program would be inadequate. This client required an accelerated transformation. Something different needed to happen.*

and an emotionally based approach was essential to achieve what the client wanted. This was a team whose members were not open with each other; they did not offer each other honest feedback. Because of the success they had enjoyed to that point, they actually had not found it necessary to be direct with each other.

The challenge was to acquire the skills and techniques to manage the human emotional side of their interactions. It was quickly determined that emotional intelligence had to be developed. People had to learn how to connect not just technically but emotionally. And they needed to feel comfortable while doing this.

Understanding that everyone was part of a multicultural organization was the only way to rise above the differences in cultures and personality. In this way a common vision and goal needed to be set so everyone could relate to them. This multicultural approach became the centerpiece of the kickoff meetings. Senior managers explained the "To Great" visionary picture of the company.

The program took much longer to design than anyone anticipated. Every meeting with the sponsors and the participants added new perspectives and new needs. It was clear that something needed to be done immediately, and coaching was determined to be the most powerful tool to support the implementation of new knowledge and skills. TMI warned the HR director and the Bulgarian company president that some employees would probably leave the program. This had to be accepted as a normal part of the process of transformation.

The commitment by the CEO of the region and the president of operations in Bulgaria was evident from day one. Leaders participated in every training session. They displayed their own vulnerability and honesty. When other country presidents in the region saw what was happening, they opened themselves up and began to support the change process by becoming fully involved.

By the time the program was designed, it had the leadership's support to be fully implemented in all the regions. Content included leadership styles, transactional analysis, team coaching, coaching skills, and integration. All the modules were supported with individual coaching sessions.

People from the different countries advanced at different speeds. Some of the managers risked working on deep personal development issues with their coaches. They did not just look at how to manage people. At the same time, others maintained a "visitor" perspective, saying "I am too busy now to find an hour for a talk with my coach." The HR manager of Bulgaria was determined to make the process available to everyone identified to participate in the program. The attitude was explained, "Everyone should get the experience and use it however he or she finds it appropriate! We cannot push people to open a door they do not want to pass through!"

The Breakthrough

After the second module was in place, results were visible, and a breakthrough occurred. The participants became more open to sharing. At the beginning, some managers did not challenge each other and did not provide honest feedback. As they had more time to spend together, to talk, and get to know each other, more understanding and tolerance of differences between people emerged.

Between training sessions, participants began to share experiences they had with their coaches. The topics of the coaching sessions became more specific, covering how to build self-awareness, how to change certain behaviors, and how to connect with others.

Progress was evident. Trust and rapport grew between team members. One manager faced a challenging moment, a tipping point in his career development and personal life. His need to control everything in his environment had been getting in his way. Through coaching, he recognized his "control issues," and he began to change. A coaching conversation provoked a personal breakthrough that helped him make the decision to move to a different town and take a different position. At the 2013 Leadership Forum held in Bansko, a gorgeous ski resort town located at the foot of the Pirin Mountains in southwestern Bulgaria, it was hard not to notice a spirit of openness and enthusiasm.

This is not to say that everything went smoothly. One country in the region saw a director and half his staff leave the company. However, no one suggested shutting down the program because of this misstep. In fact, a shift was made to focus more on team coaching for this country, thereby creating and sustaining a team in which members eventually learned to trust each other.

One of the country presidents underscored the challenges and the opportunities: "I knew, but now I am sure, that you have to be honest, transparent, and authentic with your people for both sides to be successful. Working on emotions is the most important, a quite difficult, and a lifelong objective of every leader. Leadership development is a never-ending story, and when you connect practice and knowledge, when you know that in every situation you have a choice, you open the door of trust between you and your team."

Every company that attempts a transformational process will face its own unique challenges. TMI Bulgaria's experience is that coaching and individual support, which by definition is always customized, are essential to move through these challenges.

Transformational Questions

1. Is your organization's performance at such a high level that individual coaching may be the most sustainable approach for your people to transform themselves? If so, how can you implement coaching so it is utilized and seen as valuable?

2. When you approach a transformational process of the type described in this example, how will you set up discussions to continue your process when missteps occur along the way?

3. How can you enlist and lead a team of people to invest the time and resources to create a program that will specifically work for your organization?

PART IV

Making Transformation Stick

Transformation efforts are multidimensional and therefore require a model that builds in a framework for sustainability. TMI consultants use the Five I's model to build the foundation for sustainability. The first stage is *investigation* of the current state of the organization. This must be based on a solid foundation of accurate information. Once a clear picture has been formed, the next stage is *identification* of clear objectives and preparation of a road map to get there. Your change road map needs to be "built to last," as a best-selling book spells out. The road map must involve multiple stakeholders, and it needs to be designed with a time horizon of years, rather than months.

The next state, *implementation*, will inevitably involve measurement processes, internal communication, engagement processes, and HR processes. You may have to modify your performance management system to support the behaviors that your transformed culture requires. You will make changes along the way as the process evolves. Effective implementation, and then *integration* of the process into the organization, often requires a coordinating group, led by a senior management steering group. Transformation is a navigation process, and a senior group needs to make decisions and allocate resources as the process evolves.

The fifth state is *inspiration*. Many organizational transformational processes omit one key ingredient: ongoing emotional engagement and inspiration of people at all levels. However, emotional connection is essential to making sure that a transformation sticks.

CHAPTER 19

Let's Not Forget about Tomorrow

Janelle Barlow, President, TMI US

Many organizations focus on building a great company and forget about whether that company will continue to be great tomorrow or next year or ten years from now. Designing your transformation initiative so it lasts requires careful thinking from day one. It also requires an internal sustainability champion, as this example shows.

Staying focused is easy when you are implementing a mentally stimulating and exciting change process. Implementation activities can release an enormous amount of energy into an organization. In fact, TMI often calls the tools that encourage transformation "vitamin shots." When powerful ideas about transformation are first introduced, almost everyone builds up high levels of resolve. People will say, "We're going to do this. It's definitely going to be the way we do business from now on."

The real question is, Does that energy boost last? This question will be explored in relation to a TMI US client that went beyond our wildest imagination when it came to sustainability.

This enterprise put in place several sustainability processes during the three phases of our work together: investigation and design, implementation, and the postintervention. The most important part of the sustainability plan, however, was its champion. The human resources director believed that the transformation project was the key to the company's future success. She lived, breathed, and dreamed their branded customer service initiative. This HR director, in fact, was such a champion that she has groomed several people who can now step in and take her place if she ever leaves the company.

In many ways succession planning is the true test of sustainability. The leaders of every business have to ask two questions: What will happen if our CEO leaves? Will the CEO replacement continue to support the transformation about which we have decided?

> *The most important part of the sustainability plan, however, was its champion. The human resources director believed that the transformation project was the key to the company's future success. She lived, breathed, and dreamed their branded customer service initiative.*

TMI US once worked with a nationwide client in all its fifteen locations. The client wanted to put in place a branded approach to its customer service. The implementation efforts were considerable, and the impact on the organization was significant. Almost immediately, the client could feel the impact. And this impact lasted for three years.

It lasted that long mainly because the client kept asking for additional energy to be injected into the process. TMI was happy to respond to those requests. Brand Champions were identified and set up. Once they started meeting, the Brand Champions grabbed the reins of the project and kept everything on track with very little external support from TMI US.

Then, the company hired a new CEO, who moved the organization in the direction she knew best. She had a great deal of experience with customer service herself. It was a good approach, but it was definitely different from how TMI US was helping team members understand and offer customer service. The CEO mandated that some of the language taught in the service programs was no longer acceptable. For example, TMI US had introduced its A Complaint Is a Gift concept into the organization. The CEO nixed that approach. Rather than having customer-facing staff thank their guests for feedback, this CEO rolled out a training program that taught staff to tell guests they were sorry. Moving from saying "Thank you" to "I'm sorry" was actually a big shift. It required changes in behaviors. More important, it demanded a substantially different mind-set about complaints.

Shifts of this type leave staff confused. Is it any wonder that employees adopt the attitude of "just wait and see how long this approach lasts"? This can happen even if the previous change initiative was successful. Employees stop getting behind any new approach or initiative. Boards of directors who hire new organizational heads apparently do not provide enough direction. They seem to forget the huge investment that they have already made. Many times they fail to set expectations that new leaders will build on the existing process rather than throw it out and start anew. This is equivalent to not stopping a new CEO from tearing down a just-constructed manufacturing plant and replacing it with another—no better, just different.

Employees get confused if new leadership stops traveling down the pathway where they have been walking, maybe for years. Sometimes a change in direction is necessary. Perhaps a company needs to shift the types of products it manufactures. Maybe it needs to reorganize itself to achieve greater efficiency. But when a company is attempting to solidify a culture that will support offering the best customer service, it is not a good idea to rip the culture apart and change it every time a new CEO is appointed. A better idea is to build a solid service culture and then support it. Introducing new approaches too often is a burden on service providers and does not boost their commitment to serving their customers.

> It is not a good idea to rip the culture apart and change it every time a new CEO is appointed. A better idea is to build a solid service culture and then support it.

Investigation-and-Design Phase

Our client that was so good at sustainability is a Native American gaming enterprise. The tribe has several goals. It wants to offer better and more consistent service so people will come frequently to its casinos and stay longer once they are there. A second goal is to create more staff and leadership positions for its own tribal members and other Native Americans.

This gaming enterprise hired three consulting groups to achieve these goals. The leadership team asked all three groups to meet together both formally and socially, maintain frequent communication, and make sure that all efforts were in alignment. The three consulting groups agreed to do this. It was refreshing. This meant there was no attacking each other's efforts. The consultants were to move down the same path together, building on each other's work and creating an approach that should last for years.

When designing the casino's service brand position, TMI US included a healthy percentage of tribal members on the brand team. This gave these people leadership experience in a complex process. Native Americans' voices were heard. The composition of this team also sent a signal to nonnative staff that the owners had an interest in developing their own people.

The Native American culture is more reserved than the dominant North American, white culture. When first asked to be part of the investigation-and-design phase, the tribal members were not always willing to help. They were generally not outgoing. But everyone trusted that their natural exuberance would emerge as they worked with the rest of the team. And it did. Today when members of the TMI US team return to the casino, they meet Native Americans in the casino wearing big smiles on their faces, making eye contact with strangers, and speaking up. They are on their way to becoming leaders in the enterprise.

Implementation Phase

TMI US created every part of the branded service communication effort with the long term in mind. The two-day Brand Camps that were organized were exciting, inspirational, and just plain fun. Unique language was created for this casino and its brand. The brand team devised an easy-to-remember acronym for the branded service experience they wanted their guests to experience. Each Brand Camp was finished with a rousing cheer led by existing leadership in the casino. That cheer is repeated on a daily basis at preshift meetings. It simply doesn't grow old; it energizes people each time it is shouted out.

Postimplementation Phase

The implementation phase lasted only a few days in the life of an employee. This phase, in fact, was vital because it defined on-brand behaviors. But if the communication piece of this project had no long-term implementation plan attached to it, then it would have become just a nice memory in a matter of weeks.

Instead, a team of Brand Champions began immediate work. Chosen from all departments and levels within the casino, these Brand Champions formed a strong team. Their creativity included setting up contests among departments and teams. They crafted preshift briefings that were simple, short, and fun. But these short meetings always left teams ready to approach their days with energy. The simplicity of these briefings meant no managers or supervisors could use the excuse that there was no time to focus on service.

The Brand Champions started contests; rewards were ongoing. People were encouraged to speak up when they saw behavior that was off-brand. A senior person from within the casino introduced each of the two-day customer experience programs. The CEO stood before every group and told the employees that he wanted them all to speak up if they saw him acting off-brand. And they did. He had the habit of reading his e-mail on his phone as he walked through the casino. Absorbed by his phone, he did not normally greet people—guests or employees. He changed his behavior after he got feedback, and everyone realized he was serious when he encouraged team members to make contact with those around them.

Supervisors submitted nominations for examples of best brand behavior. The awards were called "Double Bagger Awards" based on an idea presented in the Brand Camps. This meant the person had gone beyond good service and gave memorable service to a guest or a fellow team member. The CEO held regular drawings from these nominations and awarded substantial prizes on a monthly basis. Members of departmental teams created posters introducing themselves to everyone else. A big traveling trophy was awarded to the department with the best displays.

Every piece of communication, from the monthly newsletter to daily e-mail communications, was branded. Walk through any of this enterprise's casinos, and you can see promotion of the service position everywhere. The list of activities done to keep the brand alive is significant. Managers and supervisors all receive an online tool kit to access whenever they need another idea to reinforce excellent service. This electronic tool kit contains dozens of activities to draw upon.

> *Every piece of communication, from the monthly newsletter to daily e-mail communications, was branded. Walk through any of this enterprise's casinos, and you can see promotion of the service position everywhere.*

These activities have taken on a life of their own. Talented and admired people within the casino clamor to get on the Brand Champion team. Getting volunteers for new activities is not difficult.

Many of these activities had been created on an ad hoc basis after the Brand Camps. Some, however, were discussed during the investigation-and-design and implementation phases. Team members focused their attention on the future. Everyone knew that making this significant culture change was not going to be easy.

Making an initiative sustainable doesn't take a lot of effort. But it does require focus. It requires at least one person to keep pushing until entire departments take up the mantle. Such a successful branded service initiative is not hard for any company to replicate—if that is its intention. And why would it not be? But a long-term mind-set needs to be established early on. Customer service behaviors that are part of your brand demand a long view.

And what about the second goal of more positions for tribal members? That goal has been met and exceeded. Tribal members are being groomed for leadership positions. This goal is closely linked to the branded service initiative.

If you have the intention of making one change, why not link that change to a second goal? That way you can achieve both at the same time. This client demonstrates it is possible!

Transformational Questions

1. Do you always create a sustainability plan for every initiative you undertake? Who is responsible for sustainability? How can you write a plan for sustainability that is an integral part of your transformation process?

2. How is your leadership involved with making your change initiatives sustainable?

3. Does your board of directors understand how critical it is that newly appointed leaders agree to support ongoing initiatives? How can you enlist the support of your board?

4. What is your plan for encouraging collaboration and cooperation among your external consultants who are helping you with your transformation project?

5. How is your primary champion or sponsor of your initiative planning for his or her succession? Is another champion ready to take the person's place if he or she leaves? How can you make succession planning a part of your transformation initiative?

Persistence Leads to Success and Sustainability

Suman Sethi, Principal Consultant, and Sumati Malhotra, Marketing and Project Management, TMI India

Sometimes the road to transformation can be a bumpy one. But with persistence, success can be achieved, starting with a deep understanding of what needs to be shifted and why. The transformation goal then needs to be followed through with a process that is designed to be relevant, challenging, and focused on implementation. That process must be owned by all—both consultants and the client.

Transformation frequently begins with rejection and failure. In this case, it was TMI India's failure. The potential client was a midsized bank. This segment happened to be one of the most rapidly growing business spaces in the Indian economy.

This client was among the new generation of private banks in India. Its leaders made a request to several consulting companies: "We need to improve productivity and reduce attrition of relationship managers and customer service managers through effective sales and service management processes."

The TMI team was elated when it learned of the possibility. A solution for this bank could be built that pulled know-how from TACK, the sister company that focuses on sales, and from TMI, which focuses on service. The client thought it could increase sales by offering better service, and the TMI sales team welcomed the challenge of combining these two ideas. By working with both ideas, the design team could create a sustainable solution for this client.

The bank's leaders also believed that the relationship managers and customer service managers required a shift in mind-set: they needed to stop selling products and start selling solutions. They also wanted managers to leverage cross-selling and upselling financial products to their customers. They thought this could happen if their representatives created a strong service relationship with bank customers.

TMI India thought it was a shoo-in. It did not turn out quite that way.

It Was Nice Meeting You, but No Thank You

Some clients, such as this bank, seem to ask for exactly what TMI offers. On top of that, the TMI account manager had built a good relationship with his main contact in the bank. TMI was prepared, having conducted a detailed presales audit to customize its recommended solution.

Everything went well in the presentation. The sales team included the managing director, account manager, and two subject matter experts. But two hours later, the company did not find itself as one of three agencies short-listed by the client. Everyone was stunned. It wasn't the rejection that left the team members disappointed. They strongly believed they had a great solution. They were wounded that they had failed to convince the client of this.

As the team rode the elevator down to the bottom floor of the bank's building, the feeling of rejection sunk in. The TMI team is firmly committed to sustainability, to ensuring its interventions last. When transformation occurs in an organization, it frequently requires several attempts before an intervention or learning sticks. So the TMI team members asked themselves if they were willing to give up after the first failure. That's not a good approach to sustainability.

TMI India's managing director challenged the rest of the sales team to change the client's decision. He suggested that the team do a pro bono customized demonstration. They could showcase how the company takes its know-how and makes it fit the client's needs exactly.

So the account manager went back to the bank's representatives to get their agreement to meet again. Though they were surprised to see the TMI sales team again, they agreed to the plan. The entire TMI team became committed to winning the account and approached the demonstration with passion.

An Offer the Client Could Not Refuse

The sales team was stubborn. Its prework provided a deep understanding of the client's needs. Subject matter experts created a model that combined TMI's customer solution with a customized version of a selling tool that is called "FIND." FIND is a model that uses questions to drill down with the client to discover solutions: fact questions, issue/concern questions, net effect questions, and develop solution questions. The FIND selling tool was used to show the client how people's thinking can be disrupted right when they are making a buying decision.

Looks of appreciation were on the faces of those in attendance regarding what TMI was doing. The sales team was getting them to buy in the same way TMI would teach them to get their customers to buy from them.

This free one-and-a-half-hour demonstration to twenty employees brought TMI from the bottom of the list to "almost" becoming their partner of choice for the project. While there was no doubt that the client valued TMI's approach, processes, and consultant quality, the man in charge was a tough nut to crack. The bank officer must have studied negotiation techniques because he used all the standard negotiation tactics that exist. It took three months of back-and-forth interactions to seal the deal at a price that worked for both companies. The process gave TMI India a chance to demonstrate its negotiating skills, which would also be taught in the classes the consultants would later facilitate.

The experience reinforced the TMI team members' belief in their own approaches. Their passion about creating something that fit the client was difficult for them and the bank's representatives to ignore. The bankers appreciated TMI's perseverance and got to see truly outstanding customer service skills, even while the sales team was being rejected by the bank.

A Solution Designed to Last

The approach to this project was to build a framework for sustainability that included the following elements.

Diagnostics

TMI started its diagnosis to ensure that the foundation of the sales and service structure designed for the bank was based on real-time facts and insights. The investigation assessed the bank's current level of sales and service skills. It also explored the mind-set of the bank's relationship managers and customer service managers. TMI conducted thirty-five interviews and focus groups, conducted more than ten customer service audits, and went on ten joint sales calls. In alignment with the culture of the bank, a top-down approach was created. This was the only way to achieve sustainable change in the organization. TMI facilitators could not just jump in and begin working with the relationship managers and the customer service managers. The team had to start with the supervisors who were in charge across every region in India.

> *In alignment with the culture of the bank, a top-down approach was created. This was the only way to achieve sustainable change in the organization.*

TMI India's customized solution for the branch and regional managers was designed to

- Improve the productivity of employees
- Require performance discussions that tied behaviors to results
- Ensure supervision and leadership that would boost staff retention
- Be sustainable

A Certification Process That Gave Importance to the Process

TMI wanted to make sure this shift would continue long after its consultants left the bank. As a result, TMI developed a five-day sales and service certification program based on proprietary TMI and TACK concepts, such as A Complaint Is a Gift and the PRO-PAYBACK Relationship Management Process. The workshops offered were part of creating an enduring journey of learning and transformation.

The participant learning process was designed to be difficult. The final day of the certification program included written tests and three simulations for each participant. To pass, every participant was required to score a high percentage on the tests and simulations. This meant participants gave their complete attention to the learning during the previous four days.

A Blended Learning Approach That Would Stick

Not every person learns in the same way. So TMI included a variety of approaches to make sure all participants remained engaged. Banking experts were brought in to teach; TMI used more than ten learning videos programs and customized materials to ensure high-impact learning. The team also made sure the participants felt supported and rewarded. It was important that they knew an investment was being made in their long-term careers at the bank.

Building of Relationships as the Initiative Was Rolled Out

The scope of the initiative was big. Over thirteen hundred participants from all levels of the organization interacted with TMI. One of the techniques that the facilitators taught in the sales program is called "ring fencing." It means that you never allow yourself to become dependent upon just one person in a company to which you are selling. That person may leave, and then you have to build new relationships from the ground up. TMI India also lost project managers from time to time and did not want to have a new person approach the bank as if starting all over with the client. So the TMI team assigned more than one project manager to the work and also worked with a number of the bank's stakeholders. TMI did not want a loss of personnel by either the bank or by TMI India to jeopardize full implementation of the project.

Impact

This project has overachieved its set objectives. The client has seen a very clear improvement in the performance, skills, and mind-set of employees. Concrete business results include reduced attrition and increased productivity. Each participant increased his or her sales by 27 percent. Customer service scorecards of the branches jumped after the training workshops.

Bank personnel appreciate the investment the bank has made in them. Prior to their attending the five-day workshop, TMI India part-

> *Each participant increased his or her sales by 27 percent. Customer service scorecards of the branches jumped after the training workshops.*

nered with the client's learning and development team to offer e-learning, Association of Mutual Funds India product training, and Insurance Regulatory Development Authority training as a prerequisite for the five-day workshop.

TMI has been told over and over again that this process has become part of the bank's DNA. This could not have happened in the face of the initial failed proposal to the purchasing team. Fortunately, the TMI sales team went back and reinvented itself for the client. The bank was serious about its success, and TMI had to be equally serious about its success.

A sustainable solution requires both parties in the solution to be trusted partners of each other. But even more important, business results must be realized. Finally, in a sustainable process, everyone has to learn.

Transformational Questions

1. On what solid quantitative and qualitative research conducted within your organization is your transformation process based?
2. What is required to write your transformation goals so the goals enable you to track your progress?
3. What are you doing to make sure your learning and process interventions are sustainable?
4. How have you designed a sustainability component into your programs and processes?
5. Who is in charge of your sustainability efforts? What is this person's or team's responsibility?

CHAPTER 21

Changing a Culture So Safety Rules Are Followed

Victoria Holtz, CEO, TMI Latin America

Safety is a difficult concept to consistently implement. Safety regulations interfere with productivity, and as a result, not everyone follows the rules. This sets up patterns of intermittent reinforcement that make it okay to not follow safety regulations—except when senior managers are around. While this story is a wake-up call to every organization that is concerned about safety, the principles can be applied to transformation projects in general.

The outlook was not good: four major accidents in the last two years had resulted in one fatality in the plant. People were worried, sad, afraid—and careless! Every time an accident happened, workers would remind themselves of the safety rules, but then they went back to their old habits.

The plant did not have a safety manager prior to the fatality. But after the four accidents, it hired one. Unfortunately, he worked alone, as if he were the only person responsible for making the plant, and everyone in it, safe.

His first step was to research what was behind the plant's poor safety record. In his words, "human stupidity" was behind every incident. He pointed out that everyone *knew* what he or she had to do. Practice drills were held every two months. Strict rules were in place about wearing personal protective equipment (PPE). Mobile phone usage was regulated. The problem was reinforcement. This plant was not alone in its dismal safety statistics. Up to 90 percent of accidents happen because of human error according to many studies.[1]

Skirting the Rules

One of the accidents happened in the department of a supervisor who had been with the company for more than twenty years. He was resistant to all the "new" safety rules. He said, "Hey, I have been operating this machine for twenty years! Now you tell me I have to follow a procedure, use gloves, and turn the machine off completely every time a piece of metal gets stuck? This will take forever! Do you know how much pressure we are under?"

He actually instructed his team not to follow that rule as long as the head supervisor or the manager was not around. His group was measured for results, and time was crucial. Every time someone turned the machine off, it took eight to ten minutes to start full operation again. Everyone on his team felt those minutes were priceless.

> *His group was measured for results, and time was crucial. Every time someone turned the machine off, it took eight to ten minutes to start full operation again. Everyone on his team felt those minutes were priceless.*

One member of this team—let's call him "Juan"—was a young worker who had enthusiasm and a great attitude. He needed his job, so he never said no to any task. He followed his supervisor's instructions.

He had two young boys and his wife was pregnant. Early one morning, Juan had breakfast with his family. He and his wife were happy because they had just found out that the baby was a girl. They looked at the ultrasound pictures with their boys. All of them chimed in, saying what names they would like for the baby. Thinking about his morning, Juan got to the plant, turned on the machine, and started working as usual. At one point he retrieved a piece of metal without turning off the machine, as he had been told to do. The machine caught his hand and pulled him toward the hot blades. As he screamed, people around him stopped the machine to get him unstuck. Juan lost consciousness. Later, when he woke up in the hospital, he learned he had lost his right arm.

After investigating the accident, the company said he had not followed the rules. He had signed an agreement to do so during on-boarding safety training. He received no compensation and lost his job. As for his supervisor, nothing happened to him as he said he had nothing to do with Juan's misfortune.

Literally in seconds, Juan's happy day turned into a sad, life-changing one. Those are the seconds required to make a bad decision. What could he have done? Turn off the machine and get fired by his supervisor? Challenge his supervisor's orders? Tell the manager what was happening? Quit? Ask to be moved to another part of the plant? These questions ran through Juan's mind for months after the accident.

The question each of us, especially safety managers, must ask after an accident is, What would I have done in that situation? Safety transformation requires that everyone understands he or she could have been the one injured.

Here is another example that illustrates why safety is much more than just having rules in place. Marco was a manager. He had been with the company for a few months. Everybody thought he was arrogant. He typically ignored safety rules.

> *The question each of us, especially safety managers, must ask after an accident is, What would I have done in that situation? Safety transformation requires that everyone understands he or she could have been the one injured.*

Marco would walk around the plant without a hard hat or without the glasses he knew he was supposed to wear. He justified his behavior, saying in a demeaning manner, "Nothing will happen to me; I'm not a worker!" He would attack people who politely asked him to please follow the rules.

Marco's attitude is common in many companies. People act as if they are impervious to accidents. And they are—until they have an accident. But there is another problem with this behavior. Other workers see this flagrant disregard of safety rules and follow that example. People justify their own behavior: "If my boss doesn't follow the rules, why should I? If he doesn't care about safety, why should I?"

One day, the plant was expecting visitors from the corporate offices in Europe. Marco walked around the plant as he always did, without his personal protective equipment. He went into one part of the plant that was under construction. He was talking on his mobile phone as he walked hastily, and no one dared say anything to him. The workers knew how he would respond, so they avoided him. He was angry, talking loudly, because the person who was to pick up the visitors from Europe had not gotten to the airport on time. As he moved back and forth on a raised platform, he tripped and fell. His fall was only a few meters, but he hit his head on a metal tube and died instantly.

Everyone felt sad about the tragedy. Marco's death left his three children without a father, his wife without a husband, and other members of his family without a son or brother. The plant closed for a few days. Employees were shocked. "How could this happen?" they asked. Marco's story was a strong statement about how accidents can happen in an instant and why following the safety rules is important.

In most cases, the same person who suffered the accident could have prevented it, as was the case with Marco.

When TMI Mexico works in companies that want to create a safety culture, the TMI consultants usually see that silence is the biggest problem. People do not speak up, they do not say enough, and they do not reinforce regulations. People who are arrogant about safety are injured or members of their team are injured, because they implicitly believe the rules do not apply to them.

Marco's children will forever know that their father died not only because of his failure to follow the rules but also because of the silence of all the people who watched him. Yes, they spoke up for a while, but they allowed Marco's belligerence to stop them from continuing their warnings. If you had been on Marco's team and you saw what was happening, would you have spoken up? Or would you have watched and been silent as he went without a hard hat to the area of the plant that was under construction? One plant manager said, "Marco lost his life, Juan lost his arm and his job, Jane lost two fingers, and Angel, a subcontractor, almost lost his vision. What failed?"

The reality is that *all* the accidents at this plant were preventable. The company had held all the required safety talks. Banners had been put up to remind people of safety regulations. Managers had organized drills and had told people to use their personal protective equipment. They had put up a board with all the safety rules posted. They had tracked days without accidents. They had conducted safety training. Yet all this had not transformed human behavior inside the plant.

When TMI consultants began to work with this client, the team sought first to understand and analyze the safety efforts that had been taken. Understanding the root causes of the problem was essential. Evaluation of this client's safety culture would result in a customized safety program designed to transform the culture.

TMI conducted interviews with workers, listened to safety talks, analyzed safety procedures and reinforcement, and conducted safety walks. Everyone in the company was given a safety assessment to measure their attitudes. Finally, focus groups were conducted to help understand how people viewed and acted on safety.

Transformation of how people think about safety is the only way to change behaviors. Only with this transformation will safety become a value rather than a fashion statement. Safety must not be simply a priority or a "nice to have" but the way in which people work.

> *Transformation of how people think about safety is the only way to change behaviors. Only with this transformation will safety become a value rather than a fashion statement.*

The plant manager and the new safety manager liked this approach to safety. It made sense to them. After all, they had rules and training. What they lacked was compliance.

What *Not* to Do

Here are some principles that highlight how many corporations attempt to transform their safety cultures.

1. Many safety talks are boring and technical and held only because they are required. Safety is treated as a rational idea instead of an emotional idea. People tune out when the safety and health

(S&H) manager leads them through rules that they've heard before. Few participate. This reaction creates a vicious circle: the S&H manager gets angry, which results in people listening and participating less.

2. Workers sign safety agreements without reading them. They may receive a short introduction to safety when they are first hired, but new employees draw the conclusion that safety is not their first priority. No exams or interviews are conducted to make sure people understand why the safety rules are in place.

3. Safety rules are not consistently enforced. No consequences are set. If people forget to bring safety equipment with them, they're told, "Okay, just take care today and come equipped tomorrow." What is a worker to conclude with this type of managerial response?

4. Supervisors, managers, and even the plant manager do not lead by example. They do not always wear a complete set of personal protective equipment, they wander while talking on their cell phones, or they roll their eyes or become aggressive toward people telling them to follow the rules.

5. Supervisors allow and sometimes encourage workers to bend the rules, even if they would never say so on record.

6. People who point out safety breaches remain anonymous, so no follow-up is possible. If the whistle-blower's name does get mentioned, managers may say this person was just offering "friendly support." However, this is not how workers see people who speak up: whistle-blowers are denounced as snitches.

7. People can easily abuse a safety program. TMI Mexico learned of one worker who had three minor accidents. He collected payments for his injuries and earned time off from work to heal. Once, he had supposedly twisted his ankle and was given a six-week leave. During that time, he was seen playing football with his friends! Even when managers found out about his abuse of the system, he kept his job. Examples like this model the worst type of safety cultures.

8. When safety seminars are delivered, people are not required to attend. A variety of safety surveys found that as high as 65 percent of invited participants may not attend—in some cases because their bosses wouldn't let them. When the attitude is "It's just a thing done to look good with the corporate offices, to make them feel we are doing something," then a safety culture is not in place.

9. A sizable percentage of employees may feel that fate is what causes accidents. In the company described in this transformation story, 23 percent of the employees had the belief that "If something is meant to happen, it will. It's an act of God and we can't do anything about it. God will take care of us and if it's our time to go, it will happen, even if we are wearing complete PPE. Destiny is destiny—why worry then about safety programs?" If this attitude is allowed to be the dominant explanation for accidents, a safety culture is not in place.

10. Many times the rules for suppliers and subcontractors are not clear. When they are clear, these rules are not always followed. Some subcontractors resist the rules and are still allowed to enter the plant. Or perhaps the forms they supposedly read are handled pro forma.

11. The safety and health manager is perceived to be solely responsible for safety in the company.

12. Safety walks are not regularly conducted. With this client, TMI consultants in a two-week period observed over two hundred unsafe conditions and fifty-four unsafe acts. Any one of them could have resulted in a serious accident.

13. Assessments are not conducted to track people's attitudes. With its client, TMI Mexico measured high scores in six attitudes that hinder safety and medium-high scores on confusion regarding safety procedures and consequences. Nonetheless, the workers felt the company was doing enough about safety. Some said after looking at the assessment summaries, "Please don't bother us with this safety thing!"

Designing a Culture of Safety

Common and ineffective approaches to safety were presented to senior-level managers. During the presentation, the managers got involved in exercises to understand their role in changing the culture. The plant leaders were challenged and also made aware of what was specifically happening right under their noses. TMI Mexico worked on a safety culture design, and senior level managers gave their commitment to follow the program and become role models.

They were highly motivated to do something given the recent spate of accidents, all happening around the time they had visitors from their European headquarters. There was no hiding what was happening at their plant.

Their safety culture blueprint modified processes; established new rules; set metrics, deadlines, and desired results per phase; and laid out consequences and rewards for following the new "Safety Culture Map."

Once the Safety Culture Map, as the designed blueprint, was in place, the next-level managers and supervisors attended programs on how to lead and implement this map. They were given practical tools to embed a strong safety culture that would lead to zero accidents. They understood their role as leaders and safety ambassadors. And they committed to following the program not only with their minds but also with their hearts.

Then all employees participated in a program called "Safety for Everyone!" It was not a safety training program. Rather, it was the first step to a whole new way of working with safety. It was a cultural transformation on the value of safety. The program covered employees' lives not only at work but also on their way to work and in their homes. People loved the program; many said it changed their lives.

All employees participated in a program called "Safety for Everyone!" It was not a safety training program. Rather, it was the first step to a whole new way of working with safety. It was a cultural transformation on the value of safety.

To make the program live and last, a Safety Wall was created where workers posted stories on good safety practices. Many stories described how applying the safety guidelines saved them, their coworkers, or their loved ones. The stories were emotional. Emotions are normally required to transform a culture. People do not rationally think themselves into a new culture; they emotionally act themselves into a transformed culture.

TMI was also touched by the stories. One in particular grabbed everyone. A participant who attended one of TMI's seminars was obviously resistant to the whole safety program. He sat in the back of the room, arms crossed, with a defiant look on his face. His attitude changed as the seminar progressed. He thanked the TMI facilitator at the end of the workshop and said he had many things to follow up on. He told us that at the beginning of the course he was thinking, "What a bore. Another safety seminar."

He said he understood that, of course, safety means following rules. "But rules don't get followed unless people buy into a culture of safety," he concluded.

A few weeks after the seminar, his house caught fire. Because of the seminar, he had installed fire alarms in his house, bought extinguishers, and even practiced drilling his family so everyone knew what to do in case of an emergency. (And this was someone who hated drills and thought they were a waste of time.) On the Safety Wall he posted, "Thanks to this program and the actions I took, everyone is safe." He put up a picture of his family with a note: "This program saved my life and the life of my family. Thank you for caring about us!" He also put up notes from his children and wife thanking the company: "We are all alive because you cared!"

Safety transformation demands that people be ready to care. It demands that people walk safety as well as talk safety. When people demonstrate readiness, commitment, and caring, with careful reinforcement, they can create a sustainable safety program.

One story TMI Mexico always tells its participants is about how TMI US talked with a fire chief and asked about the fire department's safety program: "Do you have one?" "Of course," the fire chief responded. "We've already handled that. We have lots of safety training programs. We have checked all the required boxes." And then the question was asked, "But do the firefighters follow your rules?" The fire chief snorted with laughter and said, "Ha. You'd have to hold a gun to their heads to get them to follow the rules."

There in a nutshell is the challenge of transforming a sloppy safety culture into a caring safety culture. It can be done. And when this happens, companies achieve long-term results. It is possible to see hundreds of days without accidents.

How much is a life worth?

Transformational Questions

1. How often do you track employee attitudes about the transformation taking place?

2. How do you track whether employees are engaging in the new behaviors required of them?

3. Does your culture only set rules? Or does it also work with attitudes? How do you do this?

4. What is your follow-up on your transformation journey? Have you set milestones? What is your culture sustainability program?

5. Do you treat your training programs as rational exercises, or do you also focus on emotional aspects of the behaviors you want changed? How do you build emotions into your training program?

6. What is happening in your organizational culture that makes people not follow the rules? What are the consequences if they do not?

CHAPTER 22

Great Project Planning but Bad Coffee

Mariska Hulsewe, Jacques Dumans, Consultants, and Wim Barendregt, Managing Director, TMI Netherlands

Quick wins do happen, but new organizational habits and ways of thinking typically take eighteen to twenty-four months to become embedded. In the absence of continuing strong sponsorship, transformation projects can falter. When key stakeholders are not on board, transformation projects are more likely to fail or only partially succeed.

The TMI Netherlands project team could see hints of the client's issues early on. Budgets were overrun, projects usually went out of scope, and implementation teams were unable to meet deadlines. As one member of the TMI consulting team summarized the situation, "These guys are really great at planning and designing projects, but they are nowhere near as good at implementation. They can't even make good coffee."

Let's back up a bit. TMI Netherlands was invited to submit a proposal for leadership training to a family construction company in dire financial straits. Two other training firms, firms that had already worked with and were well acquainted with the business, were also invited to propose.

The client's Human Resources Department had provided a detailed specification describing what the training was to deliver. If TMI Netherlands responded to the RFP (request for proposal) by saying "Yes, we can do that," TMI would look like the other two competitors—which would then have the advantage because they were at least known. There was one more issue. As TMI saw it, the requested training would not correct the issues the company needed to address. The company's strategy was to "work in a more clever way." The RFP seemed to suggest that leadership training should be able to fix that issue and solve all the company's other problems as well.

Sometimes a set of fresh eyes can see things those entrenched in the system have little hope of seeing. Carl Jung, the twentieth-century psychologist, called this pattern "Innate Wisdom vs. Educated Stupidity."[1]

> Sometimes a set of fresh eyes can see things those entrenched in the system have little hope of seeing.

When you are inside an organization, you may have difficulty seeing what is not working. It is typically even more difficult to see what *is* working. In this case, the company's CEO was new to his position, and he committed to bringing in fresh eyes to look at the organization. But he faced high resistance to change.

Those who had been with the company for decades believed they could make the necessary changes themselves and did not need any leadership training. This entrenched attitude reflected just one of the company's problems: ineffective communication between top management and lower management, limited communication between office headquarters and people who actually "dug in the mud," as they called the work of the construction teams, and reserved or even hostile communication between departments.

On the plus side, the company had sophisticated technical knowledge that enabled it to place cables underground. For a long time this commercial advantage had served the company well. But other construction firms now had similar know-how, so the skill set had become a commodity other firms were offering at lower prices. Problems compounded, and the family-owned business was sold to a huge corporation that funded it for several years while it continued to lose money.

In spite of this ownership change, the business maintained its family structure. Because it was a construction company, male members of the same families worked there: brothers, nephews, fathers, and sons. The company usually hired people their staff knew because they were relatives. This company's family feeling supported a strong pride in the work as well as loyalty and commitment to each other and the organization. The employees behaved like a family, even though most did not know the cold, hard truth of their financial situation.

Because TMI Netherlands was an unfamiliar vendor bidding on this project, the team needed to offer something different to have a strong impact. It was obvious that the other consulting firms had not been successful at helping with the transformation the company required.

Breakthrough

The TMI consultants had the first morning slot to respond with their proposal. They used the early start to their advantage.

Arriving early on a gray Dutch winter day, the team carried all their supplies into the building. They set out muffins decorated with the TMI logo at each seat. The room was filled with the scent of freshly baked pastries and freshly brewed coffee that they had made. They poured steaming coffee into cups as members of the company team came in. Twelve people attended, two from the government-mandated Works Council and the balance from the company's management. On the screen was a single PowerPoint slide reading, "This is going to be dull." That was the only slide used for the next hour. As people sat down, they snickered at the message on the screen and commented on the aroma of the coffee. They were engaged.

The TMI project team welcomed everyone by saying in typical blunt Dutch fashion, "If you think this is going to be dull, we brought you cake and coffee, so at least you'll be able to enjoy yourselves." They waited a moment for dramatic impact and then said, "Please realize that when you order all your leaders to attend a two-day session on leadership—which is what you have asked for in your request—this is what will be on their minds: 'Two terrible days ahead of us. More promised change we can probably wait out.'" The TMI team became affectionately known thereafter as the Cake Guys.

The company representatives sat up straight. They could see that this group, with muffins and coffee that smelled better than anything they made, was willing to work in a different way than using PowerPoint presentations laden with bullet points. (Many of the twelve-member team saved their muffins to later give to their staff—the kind of thing you would do for someone in your family.)

In the early morning meeting, the Cake Guys shared what they had learned through interviews conducted in the previous days. They talked bluntly about how the management team was attempting to solve "productivity and implementation" issues by creating a new vision and printing it on nice leaflets distributed throughout the company. As they all knew, few staff members had read the leaflets or had bought into their transformative vision.

> The management team was attempting to solve "productivity and implementation" issues by creating a new vision and printing it on nice leaflets distributed throughout the company.

Transformation has meant different things over the years to TMI. Probably best describing our philosophy is the phrase "We transform words on a page to behaviors in action." This company was a classic case of written words and ideas that were not turning into action. With their "outside eyes," the TMI team could see that behaviors in the company were not linked to the company's values. On top of that, the company's mission, vision, strategy, and identified values were not clear.

The company's leaders believed the solution was for the managers to fix their communication with the groups reporting to them. If this "little problem" could be eliminated, managers could learn from their mistakes, and they could also make sure they implemented their well-designed project plans. As with many organizations, this company thought new skills could solve a deeply rooted cultural problem.

But people were not working together; little trust existed between the workers and management; the company suffered from a lack of communication between the multiple layers of management and the various departments. Most projects failed because of cost overruns and failures to meet deadlines.

The TMI project team illustrated how these situations develop in companies by acting out scenarios that made the company's team both laugh and squirm. The Cake Guys kept focused on the company's values and outlined a structure to achieve the change the company wanted. They warned the team that change would not be easy. The people sitting in the room had to provide their support or nothing would ever happen.

No one at the top level of the organization knew what it meant to conduct effective conversations to improve implementation, what these conversations needed to look like, and what format they needed to take. Yet they knew the gap between what they stated they wanted in their proposal request and what "good conversations" were was enormous. Team members from the client company were not capable of talking to each other in a way that improved performance or fixed mistakes. When someone did not do something well, everyone except the person who was performing badly seemed to know about it.

Project planning was done at the top levels with no input from the workers in the field. The expectation was that the project would be implemented by people at the lower levels. But that did not happen often. Operational project managers in the field did not think the people who made the plans knew how to plan realistically, and in the field, workers used dated ways of working, creating both overtime and costly overruns. Employees were unwilling to follow plans they thought would not work in the long run. This behavior caused both new hires and talented people to leave the company.

The hope that "If only the staff knew how to have the right conversations, problems would disappear" was not founded in reality. People depended on haphazard project conversations rather than focusing on the processes they were excellent at designing. Even more important, they were not learning from their mistakes.

Two years before the arrival of the new CEO, the company was having major financial difficulties. Some of the staff realized what was going on and supported cost-saving initiatives. But a larger part of the team, even those aware of the negative numbers, did not believe the difficulties were real. Few knew about the marketing challenges the company faced because of increased competition.

The Journey Begins

Not surprisingly, TMI Netherlands won the business. The company team asked for a one-day program. TMI told them that if they were serious, they needed to hold two-day programs, plus an activity involving managers visiting and interacting with the groups in the evening. Questions posed during the day would be answered by top managers in the evening. This would show a breakthrough in transparency. After a question-and-answer session, they would all go to dinner, further breaking down barriers between levels of the organization.

The company wanted the groups to be divided by rank for the training. Again, TMI resisted. The TMI team said that without mixed groups, their process would only reinforce the negative aspects of what was happening in the company. TMI also recommended training internal coaches who would continue reinforcing the new style of communicating.

All programs started with a video message from the CEO. He received coaching to deliver remarks from his heart. He talked about what he personally wanted to achieve, and he discussed what the company needed to achieve. He shared the company's history, explaining the problems it was facing in simple terms. He asked the attendees to take part in the transformation and told them he needed their help. His remarks profoundly affected every group.

The TMI project team sharpened and clarified what was going on, and then delivered a program addressing the company's issues, always linking the messages to the company's values. TMI hit solid ground by building on the pride generated by so many family members working together. Using company examples, the TMI program facilitators taught the managers how to influence and communicate with their people on a regular basis.

Managers and construction teams learned how to evaluate each other and learn from mistakes. Managers began to ask open-ended questions instead of just telling people what to do. Most conversations in the company had been judgmental and opinionated. The conversation evaluation developed by TMI was based on the company's values, which became clearer to everyone as the initiative gained steam. The question the managers kept in mind was, Were they delivering and leading from the values they said they believed in? This was a huge shift from the conversational style that had previously created resistance.

Once people began to understand the true nature of the "family's" financial situation, trust increased. Both workers and managers began to change. Workers in the field began

Managers and construction teams learned how to evaluate each other and learn from mistakes. Managers began to ask open-ended questions instead of just telling people what to do.

to take responsibility for their actions, and people at all levels operated as a more unified team. Many managers had recently insisted on new cars for themselves. When faced with the reality of the company's financial situation, they stated they never would have asked for automobile upgrades had they known the honest financial figures. These same managers who had earlier resisted change now worried they had started too late to make the essential changes.

The managers were coached for a year on how to encourage the style of communication required to build on the value strengths of the organization. They learned how to give clear performance improvement feedback, so changes were starting to be seen at the project implementation level. The coaches could see the impact. Transformation, you might say, was beginning to happen.

Coming to Terms with Yet Another Change

After a year of significant progress, the CEO who had approved the hiring of the TMI consultants was forced out of the company. Financial improvement was not coming fast enough for the owners, so they sent in someone who was also an owner. This new CEO was unwilling to fund anything he deemed an unnecessary expenditure. It was time to fix the bottom line, and this included removing funding for the TMI consultants.

"Stop doing all this nonsense" was his attitude. His opening message was, "I'll leave when I have traction." He reverted to a telling mode, and the coaching initiative went underground.

Because of the strong presence of relatives working in the company, the network continued to operate, but official openness was gone. Many talented people left. Expectations that had grown high were dashed. People could see that they had a way out of their old performance issues. Once they started working this way, they did not want to go back to a command-and-control type of management.

The TMI project team understands that transformation can occur only if the company works from foundational values when facing a crisis. When asked how they felt about their initiative being cut off at the knees after a year's worth of work, the TMI team acknowledged that sometimes you just have to let go. An outside consulting organization always has to keep in mind that external consultants do not control the situation. At a minimum, these facilitators hoped they had inspired individual managers to use a more open communication approach in their careers. As one of the TMI consultants pointed out when she heard about the number of strong people who had left the company, "You can't show people heaven while setting up barriers to entering the Promised Land. People won't wait around until the doors reopen."

In short, when attempting organizational transformation, companies should avoid showing what is possible and then returning to an experience that does not match what was promised.

Transformational Questions

1. When faced with financial pressures, how do you decide whether to continue funding change programs that have set people's expectations? If you have to stop such expenditures, how can you do it without destroying trust in your leadership?

2. How do you brief newly hired heads of organizations or departments on how to continue the messages of change programs already adopted by the company?

3. What are the risks of attempting to fix structural and cultural problems with simple training programs?

4. What are the lessons you can learn from this Dutch company?

5. What could the TMI consultants have done to head off a return to the old way of doing things?

PART V

Transforming on a Personal Level

Sometimes events happen that make us rethink about how we will live our lives, and what our aspirations are. We may be given new perspectives that help us become aware of habits that are leading us away from happiness rather than toward it. We might be put in a situation where we rise to the occasion with new confidence, a confidence that lasts for the rest of our lives. We might come across people or organizations and say, "I want to be like that. I want to join that cause!"

In this final part, we share heartwarming stories of transformations of people's lives. You never know when that transformative moment might happen. As the popular aphorism goes, "Today is the first day of the rest of your life." Enjoy the stories.

CHAPTER 23

"The Little Match Girl" Gets a New Ending

Johnny Hassinggaard Jensen, CEO, TMI Denmark

It never ceases to amaze how small changes in our behaviors can have an enormous impact. Of course, consistent implementation requires discipline. Personal transformation is never without effort. In this case the impact was the saving of a marriage.

O utside it was icy cold, the kind of cold that even the warmest winter clothing cannot protect you against. Snow was falling, and it was still dark, even though it was almost nine o'clock in the morning. Denmark's geographical position in the northern latitudes means dark winters. Participants, all from one company, entered the room and the TMI facilitator spotted one woman immediately. She looked tired and burned out. Her eyes were without life. She already seemed exhausted and it was only early morning.

The Time Manager facilitator started with a simple but funny illustration about how you spend your time results in how you live your life. Then all the people in the room introduced themselves to each other. In her introduction, the tired-looking woman said she was the office manager at one of the company's sites.

She had been with the company almost five years, and she still liked it, though she worked hard and long hours. Married, she had two small children: a three-year-old daughter and a five-year-old son. She left for work early, so her husband took care of the children in the morning. Their agreement was that she would pick them up after work. But when evenings arrived, she typically called her husband to ask him to pick up the children because she had to work late—again.

Every morning when she left home, her intentions were different. She tried hard to keep the family agreement that she would pick up the children. But as the day went by, things just happened, and she felt it was necessary to personally address one emergency after another.

She hardly dared to go home. She knew her husband would be angry and disappointed with her. She could predict what would happen. They would start to quarrel, the children would start to cry, and he would go to bed. She would stay up and work through most of the night, filled with remorse for her family and herself.

Her colleagues were not of much help. They preyed on her and said that since she was working late anyway, she might as well fix some of their problems, too. The weekdays went by fast, and before she knew it, it was the weekend.

The woman's voice trembled as she told her story. The room was quiet as everyone listened to her. It felt as if what little Danish sunlight was present had gone away. We all thought that this was serious! Lost in a maze, she was a picture of misery.

As the program went on, we discussed topics such as work-life balance and how to set priorities for both our work lives and our private lives. We talked about how to rebuild energy, plan, and avoid procrastination and interruptions and the importance of a good night's sleep. Each session we heard more and more anguish from the distressed office manager. She survived on three to four hours of sleep a night. She usually woke up a couple of times during the night as she thought of more things she had forgotten to do. All this was affecting her short-term memory.

She saw no way out of her misery.

During one of the breaks, she and the TMI facilitator talked privately. The woman knew she was in deep trouble. She could feel it inside, and she could feel it at home within her family. In the hallway, the pair recalled a powerful story known to every Dane, "The Little Match Girl" by Hans

Christian Andersen. The story is a heartwrenching tale about a poor, young girl. She attempts to make money by selling matches—hence the title of the story. When the story opens, the waif is shivering from the cold but afraid to go home. She fears the beating she will receive from her father if she fails to sell her matches. To warm herself she lights one of the matches. In the flame she sees visions of a Christmas tree and a holiday feast.

Glancing up to the heavens, she spots a shooting star. She thinks of her dead grandmother, the only person to have ever treated her with love and kindness. Then her grandmother appears before her. To keep the vision of her grandmother in place, the girl burns up all the matches.

This poignant tale has two endings. Andersen's classic ending is that people find the girl dead the next morning on the street and feel pity for her. Remarkably, this is Andersen's version of a "happy ending" because the little girl is now in heaven with her grandmother. She is warm and free from poverty. A contemporary version of the story has a different ending—a kind family rescues the girl. They give her food, warm clothing, and a nice soft bed.

The TMI facilitator and the woman agreed that this famous Danish story needed yet another ending. They wanted an ending that would give the woman more possibilities than either a future life in heaven or life with another family that would rescue her! She was not a child after all.

The woman went back into the session and worked intensely the rest of the day. She was active in the session, seemingly having found a new source of energy. After the single-day workshop, she told the TMI facilitator she was inspired. She knew there would be three individual follow-up coaching sessions with the facilitator during the next two months. She said she was looking forward to them.

As the follow-up sessions were conducted, the woman's "Little Match Girl" story evolved. She changed her productivity habits so she was able to work fewer hours than before. She set limitations on what others expected her to do for them. As a result, she created more value for herself, her team, her company, and her family. She was not going to burn up all her matches for a brief glimpse of heaven.

The woman reported feeling energized, sleeping seven to eight hours without waking up during the night. She was able to devote more time to her husband and children.

Approximately six months after the Time Manager program, TMI Denmark conducted a leadership development program with the middle management team. The woman was in attendance again and was almost unrecognizable compared to her appearance the previous winter. She looked happy and satisfied, and her eyes were alive. It was a happy reunion. She told the whole team her story and acknowledged that she was a former "Little Match Girl."

Her story now had a twist because she had written her own happy ending. She confessed that her husband had said that their relationship didn't match how he wanted to spend his life. He was ready for a divorce. After the changes she made, they were back on track.

One of her colleagues asked what and how she had changed. "Well," she said, "the answer to that is quite simple and yet requires discipline to achieve. Small changes can make a big difference! You just have to make them."

> *"Small changes can make a big difference! You just have to make them."*

She told the group she had drawn up a list of behaviors she needed to change. She even took the trouble to write down in detail why she should make the changes. She prioritized her list and started with one change in her family and one change on the job.

She committed to getting home to her family on time every day. On the job, she prioritized her tasks every day and stuck to her plan. This meant she had to say no to people at times. When she felt that the two changes had been solidly implemented, she chose two more behaviors—again, one change for her family and one change on her job. She kept doing this until each change became habitual.

The power of her transformation affected everyone in the seminar. They realized that a lot of people in Copenhagen were trying to make their lives work by selling matches. Some of them were in that very seminar room. To transform themselves, people need a helping hand plus some self-discipline to change their stories. That day was a good day for the seminar leader.

CHAPTER 24

Investing to Bring Out the Winners on Your Staff

Fransiska Atmadi, Managing Director, TMI Indonesia

How does an organization enable shy people to have the confidence to participate actively on the team? Have them share their strengths with others—their expertise—and watch them transform before your eyes.

The TMI Indonesia team got to know Stephen because he worked for a TMI client that consisted of a large group of companies. Stephen worked in Finance. Considered to be highly talented, he was one of the youngest people ever promoted to the rank of supervisor. Stephen's managers, always on the lookout for future leaders, felt that he had the potential for a bright career. As a result, although they had some reservations—because of his youth and relative inexperience— they invited Stephen to take part in an extensive leadership program designed by TMI. The program was intended for senior supervisors and advancing managers.

The lengthy program was experiential, and self-discovery was baked into its design. The company chose to locate the venue outside Jakarta in a mountainous region. They wanted to isolate the participants from daily company operations. Breaks were lengthy and a significant part of the retreat's design. Everyone would have the opportunity to get to know each other outside the work environment. Learning and development were not restricted to the seminar room.

Once all the participants had arrived, they joined a "tribe." The tribe was to be their base unit. Each tribe selected a tribal leader and designed its own tribal structure. Some tribes created loose structures. Others put a person in charge of each function, such as money management, sports, discipline, timekeeping, and fun minister.

TMI Indonesia also designed a rotating system that required changing sleeping arrangements, workshop seating, assignments, and various activity groups based on age, background, and business unit. While participants grumbled about all these changes, they grudgingly admitted the shifting landscape meant they got to work with and learn from a wider variety of their colleagues.

As the TMI team got to know Stephen, they discovered several things about him. He knew some participants from his business unit. He definitely did not yet know anyone outside Finance. If he was to advance in his career, this was the time to form relationships with people who worked in other parts of this diversified group of companies.

He was the youngest in the program, and we could tell that he did not have a lot of experience outside his specific financial area. Shy and quiet, Stephen would remove himself from the entire group whenever he could. He would sit at a small table cornered in the dining room during breakfast, lunch, and dinner. It was almost as if he wanted to remain invisible. No doubt, his youth and inexperience made the retreat a painful experience.

In the group discussions, Stephen did not contribute much to the conversation. He later said he was reluctant to show his lack of experience. He had rarely visited the company mills and factories, so he did not understand the operational challenges everyone faced in the field. Participants watched him "follow the wind," as people say in Indonesia. He would agree with everyone else. Pretty soon his tribal group stopped asking for his opinion.

His behavior seemed to say that he needed to prove to his team that he could solve problems but he needed to work on his own. He did not want to ask others in his group for input or get involved in their discussions. With his seeming passivity and isolation, his team began to ignore him and stopped communicating with him. They made important decisions without involving Stephen, which made him withdraw more.

Something had to change. TMI wanted him to be successful, so the consulting team shifted Stephen to a group where everyone was quiet. During discussions, someone had to break out of his or her personal comfort zone or everyone would sit there without saying a word and nothing would be accomplished. After some time, Stephen began to be the one who emerged. Over the next few days, this quiet group worked on exercises that demanded group consensus and decision making. Stephen became more confident in taking the leadership role in his group.

A real shift occurred when TMI facilitators changed the groups again. They assigned one person with a financial background to each group. The groups had to complete an experiential learning activity that required significant financial understanding. Stephen was one of the people with the requisite knowledge, so he became the financial point person in his group. With this structure, other members turned to him for ideas and suggestions in solving group problems. Stephen eagerly took on the role to help his team members. His young age did not seem to matter, and his confidence level visibly increased.

With transformation, once a breakthrough in one area occurs, everything begins to change. Stephen began to display changed behaviors outside the workshop sessions. He began to mingle with others during breaks. He sat at the larger tables during meals. He even joined morning sports activities. He became more accessible, and he began sharing details from his own life so other

> *With transformation, once a breakthrough in one area occurs, everything begins to change.*

people got to know him. Not only did he gain new insights from the program, but more important, he started relationships that would serve him throughout his career at this company.

At the end of the program, TMI facilitators asked the participants to nominate each other for various awards. Caught completely unaware, Stephen found out that he had been nominated for and then won two categories: the most helpful and the most positively transformed. He was thrilled.

Stephen did not become a winner, to use TMI's language, because of his participation in this leadership retreat. Rather, he already was a winner. His managers at company headquarters could see this before they invited him to attend this special leadership program. What the retreat did was to put Stephen in a challenging but supportive environment. The retreat pushed him out of his comfort zone until he could find the confidence to work with an experienced team. And then his talents could emerge, which they did.

This type of individual transformation often occurs on project teams, inside departments, or in structured learning environments. TMI has seen it again and again in seminars. This type of personal transformation is invaluable to the individual, of course, but perhaps even more valuable to the company. Without his new confidence, Stephen might have failed if placed in a managerial position or made a project leader. He might have retreated, working on his own rather than involving his team.

He then would likely have been evaluated as being out of his depth and would have reached his career peak. "Such promise," people around him would say. "Too bad he didn't realize it." The company would have concluded that they wasted time and resources on him by nominating him for this retreat. Team members who worked with him would have become disgruntled. Stephen would never have had the opportunity to show his strengths.

> You cannot predict when and where this type of personal transformation will occur. All you can do is to structure a challenging learning environment, place talented people in it with experienced facilitators around them, and trust that the winners inside will break loose.

TMI facilitators know that you cannot predict when and where this type of personal transformation will occur. All you can do is to structure a challenging learning environment, place talented people in it with experienced facilitators around them, and trust that the winners inside will break loose. There is a good chance they will. Just as Stephen did.

CHAPTER 25

Confessions of a Resistant Innovation Manager

Danilo Simoni and Alessio Cavallara, Managing Partners, TMI Italy

Your time is your life. If you make the most of your time, you will lead a rich and productive life. This story is told by a participant who went through a TMI seminar on mindfulness. He describes his transformation—and how he mindfully learned how to lead a richer life by focusing on his time second by second.

I am the innovation manager in a very successful consulting company. We work with "big data," and I am an IT engineer who works with codes and numbers. They have always driven my decisions—at least until I met some crazy guys from TMI Italy.

Our HR manager had the impression that a large number of people in our company behaved like good firefighters. We were extremely effective in resolving current problems at the source, but we generally were reactive, responding only when it was necessary to act. This method was bringing us closer to an existential crisis.

I definitely wanted more out of life. In fact, all of us inside the company wanted to be more engaged with our work. We wanted to feel connected to what our clients were doing instead of just fixing their IT big data problems.

As the HR manager searched for a consulting company to help us, one stood out. The TMI Italy consultants talked about their unique approach. They had two main ideas they would blend together for us. They would use their Time Manager results tool and also teach us mindfulness techniques. The Time Manager ideas would help us achieve long-term objectives, manage time through an effective decision-making process, and increase productivity by using a sophisticated clarification of the tasks we had to do. The mindfulness techniques would teach us to keep our attention focused on the tasks identified as priorities and resist the distraction of activities that were not productive.

I was immediately skeptical and felt that I was being asked to waste two days of work to pursue relaxation techniques. The thought of managing my time through techniques that allowed me to remain calm and silent did not thrill me at all; in fact, the whole notion frightened me. I sincerely believed that the mind cannot be calm—it needs to be constantly thinking and worrying. In my vision of the world, the mind works like a bicycle: if you continue to pedal, you move; when you stop pedaling, you fall. Everything creates thoughts and worries, I reasoned, because the mind can exist only by running after something or running away from something. In any event, it runs. In running, the mind exists. The moment you stop thinking, the mind disappears. I was brought up with certain concepts common in the engineering field, and the fear of losing them completely blocked me.

I informed the HR manager of my skepticism, and she told me that I should just try it—try as if my life depended on it. She could see my distress at work. Even after much discussion with colleagues who were also going to participate, my doubts did not diminish. But I consoled myself with the knowledge that soon everything would become clear to all my colleagues and they would discover what I had always known about mental activity. I would be right! In addition, we were meeting in Bologna where a huge beer festival was being held over the weekend. At least I would have the small consolation of being in Bologna to celebrate the end of the training program.

One month later, the course began. I remember that morning very well; the sun had begun to warm the air and the sky was cloudless. A bright room with parquet flooring reflected the sunlight that was now shining on the city. Chairs had been placed in a semicircle, and beside each chair was a training mat that I thought must be for some dreaded sit-ups.

With this in mind, I met the TMI facilitators. They introduced themselves by greeting me warmly and shaking my hand. Their handshakes conveyed strong positive energy. Their smiles and their way of making me feel comfortable made me think that perhaps, if nothing else, I would get to know two interesting professionals. We were all expecting the standard self-introduction by the trainers: "I am. . . . In my life, I have. . . . I have lots of experience in. . . ." Instead, one of them came toward us with a shiny tray that held ten cups filled with coffee—one for each of us.

The trainer said, "We are going to talk about mindfulness and time management today. Let's start by doing something according to a mindfulness idea. Taste this coffee and notice any differences compared to the coffee you usually drink. You'll have five minutes to drink this coffee and then compare notes."

I was intrigued but wondered how this could possibly be useful. When we talked, my colleagues noted how this coffee was different from traditional Italian espresso. It had a slight chocolate taste; the aroma and body were different; the temperature was not the same. It even had a different color. After five minutes, we promptly informed the trainer of all these differences.

The trainer took the floor and said, "Did you notice how your perception increases when you add awareness to your behavior? The experience you have is greatly enriched with simple awareness." He then asked, "What would have happened if you had not been asked to pick out the differences?" It became instantly clear that we would have missed the pleasure of this experience, the peculiarities of the taste of this particular drink. We would simply have become immersed in drinking the coffee without really being aware. Then the trainer asked us, "Think of your job. How many times do you just engage in automatic behavior?"

A small crack had appeared in my beliefs. Was it possible that this "esoteric" approach could uncover such practical aspects? For the first time since I had found out about the course, I began to commit myself, trying to get the most out of this experience. My transformation was starting.

The program was introduced, and we were told that we would learn tools to let our productivity explode and to manage our feelings and energy. After the first round of introductions, our needs and expectations became clear: to have the tools and the techniques with this unique approach that allow us to best manage our energy.

I began to realize the potentialities of Outlook that I had completely overlooked before. For example, by simply deactivating the pop-up that informed me of the presence of new e-mails, I could concentrate more on the activity that I was performing, thus avoiding a waste of energy and a lot of "bicycle pedaling." I could protect my time! I could channel my energy. E-mail was a choice rather than a condition of my life.

I remember perfectly the sensation at the end of the first day. The TMI facilitators asked us to do a small exercise during the evening hours—to be present and aware of ourselves. They told us to listen carefully to those whom we spoke with, pay attention to our surroundings, and let our minds concentrate on the task we were performing, whatever we were doing.

I walked through the main streets of Bologna, a truly beautiful town. I opened up to the sensations I was feeling. I concentrated on how I placed my feet on the ground. I looked around carefully and noted many details that I normally overlooked when walking. Everything was different, enriched by new sensations.

> I looked around carefully and noted many details that I normally overlooked when walking. Everything was different, enriched by new sensations.

I became aware of how my constant reactions to stimuli made me lose energy and how this took me further away from my direct experience. I did not observe or experience my environment—I merely reacted to it. In the morning, as usual, I had breakfast at a coffee bar. I noticed the same sun and the same festive atmosphere of the city that was anticipating the weekend holiday. But they were somehow different.

After arriving in the classroom, I greeted the trainers and my colleagues and proceeded to share the experiences of the night before. It was clear how my initial skepticism was replaced by curiosity and how curiosity was leading to experimentation and action.

Now I was waiting for the mindfulness techniques, which were the focus of our second day together. After a brief lecture on mindfulness technology and the scientific protocols from which it was derived, it was time to take a mat next to our chairs. We were told to lie on our backs on the mats. In a relaxed climate, we carried out three simple exercises: breath awareness, autogenic training, and visualization.

With my eyes closed, lying comfortably on my back on the mat and guided by the trainer's voice, I felt calm and relaxed. Conscious breathing efficiently oxygenated my blood and allowed me to recharge my batteries: an efficiency tool, I thought.

In the debriefing stage of the activity, we all looked around, surprised, feeling a new source of energy. We felt serene and recharged. Above all, we understood how difficult it was to remain mindful. When we continuously changed our attention, it drained our energy, and that is why we experienced so much tiredness at work. The principles of TMI's Time Manager helped us choose our priorities and plan the agenda; the mindfulness techniques softened our instinctive habits of responding automatically to various stimuli.

The trainers concluded the program on a strong emotional note—a final visualization exercise with Vangelis's "Chariots of Fire" playing in the background. We visualized the achievement of our personal and professional objectives. The trainers reminded us that either consciously or subconsciously, everyone creates mental pictures: fantasies, memories, daydreams, images, or actual films regarding our expectations or projections. Once we become aware of these images and of their effects, we can use them to our benefit to create positive sensations that help us manage our stress, anxiety, and worries in a better way and thus increase our creativity.

We said goodbye to each other—with sparkling eyes and energetic, sincere handshakes. I had learned that what is important is not what we do but the way we do it. We can do normal daily tasks but connect them to a more profound dimension of the human experience. And when we do that, everything is transformed. Our company is becoming what we call a "mindful company." Personal engagement is growing, and business is thriving. For me, I have found that every single minute of my time now has a precise meaning and purpose. That makes me a very happy engineer!

CHAPTER 26

A Goal Travels from One Part of the World to Another

Janelle Barlow, President, TMI US

Personal transformation can have an impact on our family lives and on our work lives. Such transformation can be set in motion in different ways. Read how two people had transformative aha moments in two different ways.

Papua New Guinea (PNG) is a tough place to live in and conduct business. It is also not the first place that comes to mind when one thinks of management seminars and personal transformation.

At least for me it wasn't. So when the opportunity arose to teach there, I leaped at it. After all, I was unlikely to make it to PNG as a tourist, and I wanted to see the place where, less than a hundred years ago, much of the population was so isolated they believed they were the only people on the planet.

As it turned out, I conducted at least a dozen programs in Port Moresby and Lae for the largest PNG trading company, beginning a multiyear process at a time when all the managers were either Europeans or Australians. I was invited to be part of a process to develop local managerial talent so that natives could make it to the top—right up to the level of division general manager.

My seminars were about productivity and results. This was no problem for the Europeans and Australians. I eased into the local culture by mostly learning from the nonlocal managers. But soon my programs became filled with more and more local participants, until eventually there were only one or two Europeans in a program. The locals were eager but had much to learn. Some showed up in the training classes with no shoes—not because of poverty but because it was easier to move up and down hillsides with bare feet, and shoes felt uncomfortable to them.

The opportunity for transformation was rich!

I often wondered what the participants thought of me—a white woman from California, traveling by herself and teaching management seminars. I tried to get inside the mentality of the people who, for the first hour, simply sat and stared at me as if I were an alien from a different planet. They could not believe that the beautiful Time Manager results tool they were given in the program was theirs. They would not touch the binders until I physically opened them and asked them to write their names on the first page.

Some of the stories and examples I used in the seminars were far outside the life experience of many of these people. They looked very interested in what I was saying, but I honestly did not know if they could relate to me. Cafés in Port Moresby, for example, were places where people sat and mostly ate pork under trees on picnic-type tables that teetered on hard-packed dirt. Traffic was harrowing. The unwritten rule in PNG was that if you had an accident, it did not matter if someone was injured. You hightailed it out of there because you risked your life by hanging around!

Once upon arriving at the hotel where the seminars were conducted, I called the Human Resources Group to speak with my main contact in PNG. I was told, "Oh, he isn't here." I thought the woman who spoke to me had said, "He went out to get some bread." Now, that was an unusual excuse, even for PNG, so I asked again where he was. Only after listening to her several times did I hear what she really meant, "Oh, he's dead."

The previous weekend, this highly talented man had stepped out with a crowbar to defend his son, who was being robbed in their driveway. The robbers shot the man in the head, killing him instantly. He was a superb human being and not the kind of talent his country could afford to waste.

It was hard for me to relate this culture to my own life—and what I was attempting to teach. One of our main messages in the Time Manager seminar is that everyone has only one head, and he or she carries the same head from work to home and back again. We used a lot of personal examples to make this point. I will never forget one older man who came up to me on the second day of a program and said, "I liked what you said about your husband. And I've decided that I don't pay enough attention to my wife. So I took her out to eat last night, and I'm going to do that once a week from now on." It was not the same as going to an overpriced San Francisco restaurant where the parking alone probably equaled the cost of several PNG café meals. But the principle was the same. I was thrilled.

I was learning how to talk to people who live in a culture entirely different from my own. I merely had to find an open door through which we could both walk. My personal example resulted in a man making a concerted effort to spend more time on things that were truly important to him, and this meant spending time with his wife.

After hearing several responses of this type over the years I visited PNG, I wasn't too surprised when one day a much younger man came up to me and said, "You know, I was thinking about what you said about goals last night. And I've decided that I'm going to set a goal and achieve it." I was intrigued. He continued, "I didn't know I could set a goal and then achieve it." And this from a young man who had been educated in the Australian university system, where many of PNG's young, talented people go to school! Clearly, he had never seen how setting a goal was applicable to his own life.

I responded simply, "Yes, that's true. You can do that." But while saying that, my mind was reeling. The idea of goal setting seemed so obvious to me that I think I was born knowing it. However, it was a fresh new idea on a very practical level for this young, well spoken man. So I naturally asked, "What's your goal?"

Imagine my surprise when he said, "I know that this company wants local managers to run this company. And I've decided to one day become general manager of my group." I was stunned. He was a long way from getting such a position, so it was a far-reaching goal. However, he did have the innate capability, as nearly as I could tell. He was clearly willing to take a concept and not just repeat it but also apply it to his own life in a transformative way.

> *He was clearly willing to take a concept and not just repeat it but also apply it to his own life in a transformative way.*

I knew something significant had changed in his personal perceptual system. This company was, after all, a significant force in the PNG economy. To be one of its general managers would be a crowning achievement to anyone's career.

So I hesitated (I know the power of pausing!) and stared at him eye to eye with as much intensity as I could manage. I wanted him to remember the moment. I placed my hand on his arm, grabbed tight, and said, "I believe you." I paused again and then said, "You just have to let me know when this happens, because I'm going to come back to Port Moresby to see you take that office."

He looked at me. I looked at him, and I knew a bargain had been struck. That was as strong an individual transformative moment as any I have ever experienced!

No doubt you are wondering if he became general manager of one of the divisions of the company. He's not there yet, but I track him on the company's website and believe he has the capability and the determination to get to one of the company's top positions. And it all started with a simple story from my California life about an exercise goal I set for myself. That simple example traveled across many bodies of water to grab someone with great force and personal transformative power.

That is what the transformation business is all about.

You Don't Always End Up Where You Thought You'd Be

Azmi Omar, Head, Branded Customer Experience, TMI Malaysia

Transformation is scary. It does require stepping out into space, but as this story relates, you cannot get where you want to go without taking that step.

Whthen I started working, it seemed that I was all set in my career path. My first job came after college graduation, and I thought I'd stay there forever. My future was mapped out. I was settled. At least that is what I thought. When you let yourself be transformed, however, you don't always end up where you imagined!

I first came across TMI Malaysia when I was working at what I considered my career for life. People at the very top of the organization had engaged TMI Malaysia and their colleagues from New Zealand to design and deliver a huge branded customer experience project. I was on my company's implementation team.

As the project progressed, I was assigned the task of "getting to the ground," as we called it, and influencing people who were customer facing. Very quickly, my focus changed from being profit driven, in line with the organization's objective, to being people driven. Putting People

> *Very quickly, my focus changed from being profit driven, in line with the organization's objective, to being people driven. . . . I was "putting people first"—rather than focusing on profits first.*

First is a powerful directive to any organization; it also happens to be the name of one of TMI's signature service experience programs. I was "putting people first"—rather than focusing on profits first.

I didn't know it at the time, but I, myself, was changing by spending long days with our staff, facilitating their learning experience, and making an impact on their personal lives at the same time. The work was very different from my previous job tasks. There is no question in my mind that people change based on the activities in which they engage. I stopped focusing on bottom-line activities and began to focus on what it truly meant to put people first. That key TMI philosophy addressed an issue I had always struggled with. How do you put your *customers* first if you don't put your *people* first? This project, a temporary job assignment for me, was changing my fundamental approach toward organizations and the people who work in them! Without doing anything, I was transforming right in front of my own eyes.

You can probably guess what happened. Some time after my role on the project was complete, I started to think about leaving the company. I could not quite pin down where the itch to leave came from. On the outside, everything was great. I was very well compensated. I was considered to be a high performer in my department and was reaping the benefits that came with it. I was well regarded by my supervisors and colleagues. My career was on the rise, and I was still young.

All I knew is that I had to leave and that this decision felt right. And so I left after fifteen years with the same company. In Malaysia, people just do not leave jobs like mine unless they are recruited to another position.

Two years later, I was working for another company. This new job had a huge learning curve built into it, and by all rights it should have been exciting. But I was not happy. In my heart, I knew that the job was not right for me. And a bothersome question kept popping up: Am I putting myself first? It certainly did not feel that way.

I had previously gotten to know George Aveling, the CEO of TMI Malaysia, through the branded customer experience project with my previous employer. He had heard that I was no longer with that company and called me just to touch base. Little did I know that he had been thinking about me for some time and wanted to explore my joining the TMI team!

When we met over coffee, George asked a lot of questions that triggered an awakening in me. Asking questions is where transformation starts on any consulting project. The branded customer experience exposed me to some of TMI's most positive philosophies. These ideas had affected me way more deeply than I had realized and had been imprinted on my character and personality. I now saw that I had become more empathetic; I understood people better. Previously I

Asking questions is where transformation starts on any consulting project.

had the propensity to create drama and make everything all about me, me, me. This actually created a lot of unnecessary stress and pressure for myself. I confess I am still pretty dramatic, but my drama today is about engaging others and not just putting myself on center stage. This subtle shift had a huge impact on my work as well as my personal relationships with my family and friends.

I realized then I had changed so much that I had to leave my first job and my second job as well. I no longer was aligned with how I was spending my time at work. A lot of people could see this, including George Aveling, even though I could not.

During that conversation with George, I had an epiphany. I came to see my life's purpose: making a difference in other people's lives. I had unknowingly been doing this while involved in the branded customer experience project. But that was over, and now I wanted more. I wanted to make it my life's purpose.

My work as a consultant for TMI Malaysia, which started in 2010, has been a transformative journey. This is where I am now. I have become someone doing something I did not even know was possible. Finally everything feels right, and that is what I have come to understand that transformation is all about.

CHAPTER 28

The Power of an Aha Moment

Octavian Pantis, Managing Director, TMI Romania

How do you go from working long hours and also running over fifteen thousand kilometers while training for and competing in marathons around the world to being a blogger with over a million visitors? Simple! You transform your life by making a few changes in the rules by which you live!

The briefing looked deceptively simple until its full implications sank in:

An Antonov-74 jet will fly you to an international North Pole Camp called Barneo situated between 89N and 90N, drifting in the high Arctic Ocean. The Antonov will return to collect you approximately 36-48 hours later. Soon after landing you will be taken by helicopter to 90N, where the North Pole Marathon takes place.

Once he got there, Andrei Roşu recalled: "I wasn't sure whether I should start or not. The winds were devastating. The temperature was minus twenty Celsius, with a RealFeel of about minus thirty-five. But when I heard the start gun shot, I moved forward without hesitation. We took eleven laps around the four-kilometer circuit marked with flags on the ice. Most of the time, those orange flags were all I could see around me. In some places the ice was thinner and I could hear it crack under my feet. In other places some of the contestants were knee-deep in snow. And sometimes the wind was so strong in my face that every step felt like I was pushing a car."

Seven hours, fifty-three minutes, and fifty-eight seconds later, Andrei finished the race and with it the first step of what would become a verified *Guinness World Records* achievement: seven marathons and seven ultramarathons on seven continents—all within 582 days.

"I didn't do it for the Guinness book," Andrei said. "There are people who ate eight hundred peppers or stood on just one foot for days. If you want to get in the record book with something, you can. All I wanted was to make a change in my life—to start to organize my time better, to give up television and to run, to be a better model for my kids, and to be a better person. I didn't think I'd have a story to tell."

How did Andrei's remarkable personal transformation start?

Andrei was a successful corporate employee in Romania. He used to live a pretty typical corporate life: staying very busy throughout the day, missing meals or fixing his hunger with fast food, falling asleep in front of the television in the evening, or just browsing channels. More than once he felt the need to change his lifestyle. One time was when his son sat next to him on the sofa and started zapping through channels, just like his dad. Several other times he thought about changing when he needed to buy larger clothes, having put on ten kilos (close to twenty-five pounds) in just a few years.

One day he attended a TMI Time Manager workshop. It was the third time his colleagues from HR had scheduled him to attend it. Twice he was, of course, too busy with work to go to the seminar. Once in the classroom, he quickly realized that if he did not immediately apply what he had learned, he would never do it. So he called his wife and said, "I'll be late tonight. I need to get some things done." Then he added with a smile, "Don't worry, I'm not seeing anyone."

At three in the morning he was still in his office—very tired but happy. No icons remained on his computer desktop. His desk was clean: all documents had been filed, grouped by the categories he had set up in the seminar. His in-box was empty, with e-mails moved to dedicated folders or converted into tasks and placed on his calendar. "I can't describe the freedom I felt," said Andrei.

He then took this discipline to other areas of his life, setting rules for himself and following them consistently. He woke up earlier and did something valuable right away—reading, preparing an important report, or jogging. He took no phone calls or e-mails before 10:00 a.m. He stopped checking e-mails throughout the day and started looking at them only two to three times a day. He put everything he wanted to get done on to-do lists. He cleaned his desk and cleared his in-box and computer desktop at the end of every day. He wanted to experience what it was like to start his day with nothing remaining from the previous day.

"The first step is the hardest," said Andrei. "There are plenty of excuses lying around, waiting for you to pick them up and hide behind them. The first weeks are hard. It's important to remember why you're making these changes. You can't just jog because some other people do it." He added for emphasis, "You need to have your own goals."

> "The first step is the hardest," said Andrei. "There are plenty of excuses lying around, waiting for you to pick them up and hide behind them. . . . It's important to remember why you're making these changes."

Andrei's first running experience was a half marathon. A friend he met at the event sent him, as a joke, the link to the North Pole Marathon. Surprisingly, the North Pole Marathon struck a sensitive chord in Andrei. It felt like the ultimate adventure. He recalls thinking about the Jules Verne books he had read as a child. And he also remembered that long ago he had recurring dreams of traveling to the North Pole. The thought didn't leave him, so he began to plan a training schedule that could take him there.

"The greatest challenge was to manage my time," Andrei recalled. "I knew I did not want to merely swap one addiction, work, for another—jogging—and still be away from my family. So I chose to run in the morning, setting my alarm clock for 5:00 a.m. I knew that if I could do this for a week, I could do it for as long as it takes."

Since setting the world record by running marathons on every continent, Andrei has run marathons, ultramarathons, Iron Man events, the Double Iron Florida (7.6 kilometers swimming, over 4 miles; 360 kilometers biking, about 225 miles; and 84.4 kilometers running, about

52 miles—in thirty-five hours), and the Mexico Triple Ultra Triathlon (just imagine bigger numbers here). The distances and times are mind-boggling. And, he also finished the Virginia Quintuple Ultra (19 kilometers, or 11 miles, swimming; 900 kilometers, or 560 miles, biking; and a mere 210 kilometers, or 130 miles, running). Andrei's family is great; a second child arrived in 2011. His work is more than fine. Andrei has a blog site (www.andreirosu.org) that has attracted almost one million visitors since 2010.

He estimates he has run over fifteen thousand kilometers (close to ten thousand miles) so far, and he plans to run more. His belief in himself started with that transformational aha moment in a TMI workshop. There he realized that putting things in order was a good idea; the energy he felt after that led him to his first half marathon, which was followed by the North Pole experience and then the Virginia Quintuple Ultra. His widely read blog was born in the midst of all this running, swimming, and biking.

Do we at TMI claim we had any contribution to his successes—even 1 percent? We probably could. But we do not. We believe Andrei's achievements are 100 percent his own. After all, we did not run a single step along with him. We just did our job, which is more than delivering fundamental productivity ideas to participants. What we did was to inspire Andrei to make the most of his days. He was obviously quite capable of running on his own. We just created an opportunity for him to have an aha moment.

Should all of us run marathons on the top of the world? Probably not. The North Pole would get a bit overrun. But we all have our own fields where great achievements and personal transformations await us. We believe it is possible to get to that moment of unusual accomplishment if we begin with a few confident steps, stay away from naysayers, and avoid the obstacles that reside within us.

CHAPTER 29

My Turning Point—Transformation inside a Seminar!

Meltem Şakarcan, CEO, TMI Turkey

When someone makes a transformative decision, it may look like a simple change to outsiders. But, it could take years of preparation to get to the point where major transformation is possible. But, once that point is reached, the doors of possibility fling wide open, as this story exemplifies.

Most people celebrate their birthdays on an annual basis. I also celebrate every year the date when I began my dream job—and not because the company reminds me. I do it because I do not want to ever forget what it took to make that happen.

As far back as I can remember, I have always thought of myself as a free soul. People talk about thinking outside the box. I wanted to live there. My father controlled every aspect of his career. He was a powerful, ethical man and had an impact on a huge number of people. For me, he was my hero. I wanted to be just like him.

After graduating from university, I started in the banking sector. Not exactly in my father's footsteps, but I was not thinking much about my dream job right then. I just wanted a good job. I landed a position at a boutique bank in Istanbul, worked in operations, and was proud to be successful in my first career appointment. After all, many of my friends were not as lucky.

Then my career path made a right turn back to something resembling my father's career. After attending a presentation-skills seminar run by

TMI Turkey, I began to connect with a younger, more creative version of myself. The TMI program facilitator was impressive. She looked professional, she was sincere, and she completely managed the experience for all the participants. I pestered her with questions during the break and learned that she had become a TMI program facilitator a little late in life, but she made it clear that age was not the defining variable in being a great facilitator.

I immediately started applying the speaking techniques I was taught when I trained my team at the bank, and my seminars began to receive top ratings. Even I was impressed! I covered customer relationship skills, project management, and technical operations skills. I learned how to project empathy in front of a group—and my participants opened up so that what I taught seemed to stick more than in the past.

A growing feeling began to keep me awake at night: perhaps I was ready to become an independent facilitator. Even though I suspected I was ready, I was not quite at the point where I felt confident enough to jump out of my "job" box at the bank. So I applied to work in the bank's training department—a risky decision, indeed, for someone who by this time had years of experience in operations. Luckily, my managers could see my passion for training and I got the transfer I requested.

While in the training department, I was able to participate in the seminars of a large number of Turkey's public training companies. I learned from them all. But the TMI programs continued to have a different type of impact on me. I definitely wanted to be a part of this experience. TMI's consultants were topnotch in delivery, and they could light up a room so that deep learning took place. I could see people transform right in front of me.

But I faced two issues. First, none of the TMI managers were aware of my decision! Second, I thought there might be ethical reasons not to approach them because of my existing banking job. TMI never recruited trainers from client companies. So clearly I had to do something. I plunged ahead and resigned from the bank. While I had no more ethical issues, my family thought I was crazy and irresponsible. Here is a good learning point: when your family thinks you have gone nuts, you are probably on a transformational path!

After a few months (to avoid any appearance of impropriety since my most recent employer was a TMI client), and carrying a lot of nervous energy, I talked with several TMI managers in Istanbul, telling them I wanted to be a freelance training consultant. I could not dig up enough confidence to come right out and say I wanted to work for them. But after a test presentation, I was made an offer I could not refuse—a TMI sales manager with the opportunity to also conduct seminars on the weekends. The date: March 19, 2004, three years after taking that first TMI seminar. As they say, the rest is history.

My friends called me an overnight success, but this was not entirely the case. The pathway to dreams and transformation generally takes a little longer to travel than anyone anticipates, and it is not always in a straight line. I sold during the week and delivered seminars on weekends. This lasted for four hectic, exhausting, but personally rewarding years.

> The pathway to dreams and transformation generally takes a little longer to travel than anyone anticipates, and it is not always in a straight line.

In mid-2006 I was appointed general manager of one of the business divisions in the company, and then in 2009 I was named CEO of the sales group.

Some of the lessons I have learned while at TMI sound so simple, but they have transformed my approach to selling, training, and interacting with people. For example, you can trust me when I say I am going to do something—you can absolutely count on me. I have learned how to take responsibility for my life. When I face any kind of problem, I immediately look for solutions and do not get caught up in blaming and remorse. I no longer talk about "me" but rather about "we."

Transformation is not always about organizations. Yes, I went to my first presentation-skills program to get better at my job. That is true of probably all people attending seminars offered by their employers. And I did get better. But what I learned about transformation is that a personal turning point can also happen—right inside a workshop.

My transformation is not over yet. But I now appreciate that many people come to our TMI programs who are just as I once was. I look for eager faces—a sign they are waiting to start their personal transformation. It is a humbling thought.

CHAPTER 30

You Just Never Know

Janelle M. Barlow, President, TMI US

Personal transformation does not have to involve enormous change. A little variety in life can open doors that invite larger transformations. As these two examples demonstrate, such differences can impact our personal lives as well as our work lives.

To most people the idea of transformation sounds complex. It can be! How do you break a big concept like transformation into small, bite-sized components that are more within everyone's reach? One way to do this is to practice variety, making small changes in everyday behaviors and routines.

This chapter includes two stories about how taking simple actions to create variety can have life-changing transformational impacts. Both stories point to what can happen when someone commits to trying something new and then observing what unfolds. It is like closing one door and opening another to see what is there.

> Taking simple actions to create variety can have life-changing transformational impacts. Both stories point to what can happen when someone commits to trying something new and then observing what unfolds. It is like closing one door and opening another to see what is there.

In one of our signature customer experience training programs, Putting People First, we talk about fundamental attitudes that affect service and change. We call one of these attitudes "Change and Variety."

In order to achieve "big change," which has a goal attached to it such as losing weight, you have to set up a plan and be systematic about following it. But there is another side to change. We call that "variety."

We encourage our participants to consider ways of doing normal things differently: how they greet people, what they say to themselves when they first wake up in the morning, how they smile at people, the route they take driving home in the evening. There are dozens of such examples.

We even throw in some crazy suggestions, such as sleeping on the opposite side of the bed or, to be even more challenging, putting your head where your feet normally go. We recommend eating your food in the opposite order: start with dessert! There are no limits to the examples we can use as illustrations to how you can shake up your world.

The first story has been told thousands of times in the TMI network—in workshops and keynotes. It has its origins in a Putting People First experience delivered to airline personnel by TMI UK. When the trainer came to the "Change and Variety" section in the workshop, he suggested that the participants should go home that evening, or whenever they would next be at home, and enter the house through a different door.

One person piped up, "But what if I have only one door?"

The trainer cheekily responded, "Well, then go in through a window."

Again challenging the trainer, the person asked, "But what if I live on the second floor?"

And the trainer retorted, "Well, then get a ladder, climb up to the second floor, and enter through the window."

Now, these examples are given only in jest. Everyone enjoys them and we get a lot of laughs. Honestly, we would never seriously suggest that someone should actually get a ladder to enter the house by climbing through a second-floor window.

As it turns out, however, this young flight attendant decided to take us up on our suggestion.

She did, in fact, live in a second-floor flat and had access to a ladder. She got it out, propped it up against her building, and climbed in through an open window.

A little later, she heard a knock on her door. When she opened it, a London bobby was standing there. He asked, "Is everything all right?"

"Yes," the flight attendant responded. "Why do you ask?"

"Well," he said, "we had reports of a robbery taking placing in this building. Someone had climbed up to the second floor on a ladder, and we just wanted to check to see that everything was okay."

She laughed. "Oh, that was me."

"Hmmm," he said hesitatingly. "Why did you do that?"

The flight attendant responded with a bit of embarrassment. "Oh, I was in a workshop today on customer service, and they told us to try something different, and I decided to enter my flat by way of the window."

The bobby laughed and remarked, "Really! What else did they talk about?"

She said, "Lots of things. It was very interesting, quite unusual."

The bobby then said, "Well, I am just about to go off shift, and was thinking of going down to the pub at the end of the block and getting a pint. Would you be willing to join me? I'd like to hear more about this program."

The flight attendant did.

And the two of them eventually got married.

In our second story, I was conducting a workshop for senior managers in Hong Kong and told them the story of the flight attendant and the London bobby after encouraging everyone to put some variety in their lives. I told the leaders of this major logistical firm that they should try something different that night and share what happened with the rest of the group the next morning.

The next day everyone returned with his or her variety example. One man said that he decided to spend time helping his son with his homework, something he did not normally do. It was a very tender story, and everyone was touched. And he said, "I realize how important this time is with my son, and I'm going to do more of this."

Several other examples of this type were offered. The top managers laughed and applauded at the power of these variety stories.

And then one last person walked up to the front of the room to tell her story. She said she had decided to take the bus to work that left from the opposite side of the street from where she lived. While she was waiting for the bus to central Hong Kong, she saw a Chinese bakery she had not previously noticed because she always took a different bus on the opposite side of this busy Kowloon street.

She had a few minutes to wait for the bus, so she decided to go in and take a look at what the bakery had to offer. She said she bought egg tarts, which everyone in Hong Kong loves. She opened the bakery box and personally handed an egg tart to everyone in the workshop.

They were still warm. We happily munched on them.

While we were eating, she told the group that the workshop had so impacted her that she decided to tell the leaders some very exciting news. They would be the first to know. Not even her husband knew, though that would be the correct way to share such news, she acknowledged.

She had called her doctor's office a few minutes before the class started—and learned that she was pregnant with her first child.

She beamed. People in the class had tears in their eyes. Several came forward to give the woman a big hug. And a real team was formed in that moment of a shared variety experience.

CHAPTER 31

Learning to Be an Effective Leader Demands Personal Transformation

Adriana Mendoza, General Manager, TMI Colombia

Leadership transformation starts with personal transformation. But if an organization wants strong leaders, those people have to take certain risks in their personal lives. And when the CEO challenges people to "rise and shine," they are more willing to take those risks.

Imagine you are in a room with thirty-nine other potential top leaders within your organization. You have been assigned to attend a leadership academy. While that sounds interesting to you, you are worried about a big project that will not have your leadership while you are away from the office. You are thinking that perhaps you can get some e-mails done during the sessions. You are also a little worried about the child you left at home this morning with a cold that is getting worse.

The president of the company in your country opens the leadership academy with a short speech. He says clearly, "I expect forty people to rise and shine. When I retire, I want good leadership in place. And I suspect it has a lot to do with what you will learn in the next few months." With these words of introduction, TMI Colombia started working with forty people, helping them to be better inspirational leaders.

The academy was scheduled over a nine-month period with regular sessions over that time. As the course progressed, the participants came to see that developing leaders in their company meant they had to change themselves. Leadership as taught in this academy was not going to be just a bunch of techniques that would become action plans that no one followed. The participants learned that leadership is not something you turn on or off depending on what you are doing. Leadership is about who you are at your core.

This different way of looking at leadership produced significant personal transformations. Some were surprising. But every transformation was significant to the person who changed in larger ways than he or she had anticipated.

Example 1: Leaders have to understand transitions. A divorce is never easy for anyone, even if you do not want to be married. This kind of personal breakup represents a huge shift that typically affects people in every part of their lives. The first transformer came to a big aha moment when she began to see her divorce as a positive change in her life. She came to an even bigger aha moment a little later. She saw that leaving her last job to come to her current company was exactly the same—a difficult but important positive change.

She told the group that being a good leader meant transforming events that feel like failures into the successes they are. This is particularly true when these so-called failures open up new doors to a different life.

This woman pronounced that she was no longer going to lament what she thought were failures. She would become the type of leader who looked for the possibilities in all her transitions. And she would help her team do that as well.

Example 2: Leadership may mean jumping into a void. One of the participants shared personal regrets from not speaking to his father for fifteen years. Rather than let another night go by holding on to a self-limiting position, he swallowed his pride and called his father. They repaired the breach on that very first telephone call.

This participant learned that leadership is not always easy or fun. Sometimes leadership means taking a step into the void. Leadership is a step, he later told his colleagues, just waiting to be taken. "But you can't hide your own emotions, both love and pain," he said. "Because only through taking that leap will you know what you are capable of."

Someone quoted the proverb "If you are not living on the edge, you are taking up too much space." And that statement became the mantra for the group.

Example 3: Who you are as a person is who you are as a leader. In one of the leadership academies that TMI Colombia facilitated, a manager and one of his direct subordinates were in the same group. One of the exercises TMI conducted involved asking participants to push each other to be better than they normally are in their lives. The boss and his assistant were paired for the exercise.

Upon completion, the subordinate said, "I have a friend who has always demanded a lot from me. Sometimes that is hard, but I keep holding on to this person as a friend. Now I no longer see my boss as a boss but as a friend—a friend who just wants to see a better version of me." As he said these words, he then hesitated as if hearing what he had just said for the first time. He then added, "I guess I'll be a better leader if I am one of those kinds of friends to my team."

Example 4: If your actions inspire others to dream more and do more, then you are a leader. The Latin American human resources manager, the main sponsor of the leadership academy, told us she invited her daughter, son, and mother to build their own dream maps, an exercise introduced at the beginning of the leadership academy. She inspired her own family to connect with their personal dreams and understand what they wanted from their lives. Upon hearing this, many people in the academy followed her example and did the same exercise with others at work and at home. One participant said, "I discovered the humanitarian side of leadership. Seeing true happiness when people reconnect with their dreams has been priceless."

Example 5: Being a leader is being a positive example to others. At the last session, all the participants delivered a prepared presentation about their evolution in the leadership academy. Soon after they finished their speeches, TMI told them a gift was awaiting them. Their team members back at work had been videotaped talking about how their bosses had changed over the previous nine months. The affirmations were inspiring, personal, emotional, and unforgettable.

It was then that everyone realized the impact his or her personal change had had on others. There is a big difference between talking about yourself and hearing other people talk about you. The participants could see how they had become inspirational models for others.

Soon after the leadership academy ended, seventeen of the forty participants were promoted to new strategic leadership positions with better salaries and stronger career plans.

Transformation lies dormant in us all. But it needs to be awakened to create effective leaders. It requires inspiration and a safe environment for it to come alive in everyone.

CHAPTER 32

When Your Back Is Up against a Wall, It Can Be a Great Time for Transformation

Tunde Rotimi, Head, Business Growth, TMI Nigeria

Sometimes a challenge is the best way to bring about transformation. This example describes a dramatic shift that occurred when a bank manager found herself at risk of losing her job—twice—and used the situation as impetus to reinvent her approach to customer service.

In 2009 the ripple effects from the global economic crisis were taking a toll on the Nigerian economy. Worst hit were the banks, and they were hurting badly! Branches were shut down and layoffs were very much in vogue.

Sitting on her chair, the branch manager of one of the five biggest Nigerian banks picked up a remote and set the air conditioner for the coolest temperature—because things were heating up. She had just received an e-mail from the bank's headquarters. If her branch did not meet its third-quarter target, her branch would be shut down and she would lose her job.

This branch manager had always been passionate about making people happy. When she became a branch manager, she had an ambition to develop a customer experience that would delight all her customers. However, routine activities and bureaucratic red tape hindered her aspirations. The result was that her branch was like any other branch.

It faced long queues, a demoralized team, and not many smiles on the faces of customers as they walked out of the branch.

In 2004 she was a training manager at the bank. She managed several training vendors and spearheaded a number of transformation initiatives. One day, she received an e-mail inviting her to the bank's headquarters, where she was informed that she was being moved to the sales team at one of the regional branches. She was told it would be a new and exciting challenge. In reality, however, the targets were set very high, and each quarter they were reset to even higher levels. Quarter after quarter she missed every target. She sensed that if she did not turn things around soon, she would be out of a job before long!

> When she became a branch manager, she had an ambition to develop a customer experience that would delight all her customers. However, routine activities and bureaucratic red tape hindered her aspirations.

Around that time, this beleaguered salesperson received a notice from the bank's training department, the same one she used to help manage, to attend a five-day Branded Organizational Culture training that TMI Nigeria was running for the bank. At first she was annoyed: "Five days away from the bank, and it's not going to get me any closer to meeting my target. Gee, thanks." She placed a call to her boss, complaining about the burden this workshop would place on her. "Sorry, but it's mandatory," was his response.

A week later, she was in attendance at the seminar—not happy, but definitely there. During that program, her natural talent for service was sparked. She really liked the Complaint Is a Gift concept, whereby, instead of avoiding complaining customers, she could turn complaints into gifts, delight the customer, and build trust and customer loyalty. She also learned how to process customer requests faster by working with other departments in the branch to speed up operations.

Back on the job, she designed a customer engagement and management approach that helped her sales skyrocket. She was not just bringing new customers into the bank; the amount of referrals she got was a bank record. In Nigeria, where the customer experience has not been a priority to organizations, she became something of a service guru. In a year and a half, she was promoted to branch manager. Slowly but surely, this position dramatically drained her service spirit. She faced what seemed like a bottomless pit of paperwork. Managing over twenty people consumed the rest of her time.

In the middle of one of her sleepless nights, she remembered that five-day seminar and how the ideas had transformed her approach to customer service. The next morning, she got straight to work. She dusted off her old TMI participant workbook and started to map a way out of her dismal situation. Her plan: keep existing customers by creating a unique experience that would make her branch more customer friendly, and get new customers through the power of word of mouth. She assembled a team of three. Together they designed a customer experience framework that literally transformed the service culture in the branch—almost overnight.

Not only did her branch meet its third-quarter target. She and her team became the model for in-branch experiences for the bank nationwide.

In fact, not only did her branch meet its third-quarter target she and her team also became the model for in-branch experiences for the bank nationwide. This started a customer service competition between the big five Nigerian banks. It all started with a huge challenge, one woman's commitment to service, and a little TMI magic!

From "Ugly Babies" to Transformation

George Aveling, CEO, TMI Malaysia

I n his book *Creativity, Inc.: Overcoming the Unseen Forces That Stand in the Way of True Inspiration*, written with journalist Amy Wallace, Ed Catmull, president of Pixar, said that every movie the studio has made started out like an "ugly baby." At the beginning, it's a new thing that is hard to define; it's not attractive, and it requires protection from the naysayers who fail to see its potential or lack the patience to let it evolve.[1] Imagining the possibilities requires a shift, as we suggest in the book title.

The concept of the ugly baby is a great metaphor when we zoom from the big screen of movies to the theatre of corporate transformation. In this world, the ugly baby is a core idea. This core idea might be how to create an engaged and higher performing organization through a different style of leadership. The shift might be around differentiation through customer service. It could be about unleashing the power of customer intimacy—getting to know our customers better—by first collaborating better inside the organization. Or the shift might be around creating emotionally or physically safe environments or seemingly simple (but not that easy to implement) concepts such as a smile. The list of themes in our corporate theatre is wide and varied!

And we know, right from the start, that the ugly baby will need to be protected and nurtured. We know that, just as in a movie, there will be drama. Certain forces will want to kill off the ugly baby. There will be challenging scenes when those leading the transformation—the leadership team—may not see the same picture. What they do—or what they do not do—can certainly harm the health of our core idea, our ugly baby. We will face the natural and powerful resistance of many people who, in their comfort zones, will ask, "Why do we have to make this shift?" This is a powerful force that can kill the baby.

Yes, we have encountered many ugly babies during our time in the transformation space. The challenge—the art and the science—is to find a way forward, to grow and nurture the core idea—so that it grows stronger and becomes more attractive to those within the organization.

Catmull said that growing the ugly baby is a lot like raising a child. It's complex and interesting—and people want to make it simpler than it is. We are sure that this resonates with those who have had children and have had ideals of what their babies will be like when they grow up. We might be able to read books on how to raise our children, but it's never that easy. We learn as we go as we treat each child as an individual.

This is what happens when we embark on transformation projects within organizations. We start with the core idea—the ugly baby. We make plans for shifting based on the best information that we have available to us. Then, during implementation, we learn new things. We will come to understand that some messages resonate better than others. We may find waves of support that we can ride on. Or we might find that the planned approach is not resonating and is not nurturing the growth of the idea. We will discover detractors. We have to adopt the roles of strategists, communicators, influencers, problem solvers, and diplomats, continually shaping the shift process. We learn as we go, modify as we go, and evolve the process as new information is received.

All of this takes a lot of belief, energy, and emotional resilience!

Those involved in successful transformation efforts experience joy in initial small gains. We become energized when we see that the ugly baby is no longer perceived as ugly by some managers and team members, who start to think, behave, and shift in different ways. Passions are ignited, spread slowly, and then build momentum over time. Leaders begin to work differently and interact with their teams and the organization differently.

The joy will gradually build to elation when a new normal, in terms of behaviors, takes hold in the team or the organization. The idea—the once-ugly baby—has grown up, has become accepted, and has become attractive. People in the Finance Department shift their behaviors toward their customers. Leaders adopt a different style. Complaints are handled with a more positive attitude. Organizations become engaged with the idea of creating great customer experiences. Quality managers shift their mind-sets from focusing on procedures to focusing on people. The list goes on.

Is transformation easy? No.

Is it complex? Yes.

Does it take enormous amounts of belief and strength? Yes.

Is it worth the effort to nurture our ugly babies? A resounding yes. Few joys in life are greater than being able to look back, at times battle scarred, and say, "We stayed true to the course—and we made a difference." We shifted!

We wish you great success in your journey of nurturing your ugly baby and, in the process, making a difference in the lives of individuals, teams, and organizations.

Notes

Introduction

1. See, for example, Nitin Nohria and Michael Beer, "Cracking the Code of Change," *Harvard Business Review*, May–June 2000, https://hbr.org/2000/05/cracking-the-code-of-change/ar/1).

2. While this quote is cited in many forms, including "Culture eats strategy for lunch," Peter Drucker actually said, "Culture eats strategy for breakfast." Curt W. Coffman and Kathie Sorensen, *Culture Eats Strategy for Lunch* (Denver: Liang Addison, 2013), front flap.

3. Jack Trout, "Peter Drucker on Marketing," *Forbes*, July 2, 2006, http://www.forbes.com/2006/06/30/jack-trout-on-marketing-cx_jt_0703drucker.html.

4. Tony Hsieh, "Your Culture Is Your Brand," *Zappos Blogs: CEO and COO Blog*, January 3, 2009, http://blogs.zappos.com/blogs/ceo-and-coo-blog/2009/01/03/your-culture-is-your-brand.

5. Quoted in W. Warner Burke and William Trahant, *Business Climate Shifts: Profiles of Change Makers* (New York: Routledge, 1999), 95.

6. Steven Prokesch, "Competing on Customer Service: An Interview with British Airways' Sir Colin Marshall," *Harvard Business Review*, November–December 1995, https://hbr.org/1995/11/competing-on-customer-service-an-interview-with-british-airways-sir-colin-marshall.

Chapter 2

1. This is a description of the first edition, which was published in 1996; the second edition has a different cover. Janelle Barlow and Claus Møller, *A Complaint Is a Gift: Recovering Customer Loyalty*

When Things Go Wrong, 2nd ed. (San Francisco: Berrett-Koehler, 2008).

Chapter 7

1. Janelle Barlow and Paul Stewart, *Branded Customer Service: The New Competitive Edge* (San Francisco: Berrett Koehler, 2004).

Chapter 18

1. Jim Collins, *Good to Great: Why Some Companies Make the Leap . . . And Others Don't* (New York: Harper Business, 2001).

Chapter 21

1. "Human Factors Cause Most Accidents at Work," *NewsDay*, July 12, 2012, https://www.newsday.co.zw/2012/07/12/2012-07-12-human-factors-cause-most-accidents-at-work/.

Chapter 22

1. Many sources place this archetype with other Jung archetypes, for example, "Archetypes," Google Docs, https://docs.google.com/documentd/1rmOV3lR3uJYMVP17N8jiSbv-2a_mTSI14ABVxQ91JJU/preview?pli=1.

Epilogue

1. Ed Catmull, *Creativity, Inc.: Overcoming the Unseen Forces That Stand in the Way of True Inspiration*, with Amy Wallace (New York: Random House, 2014), 131–132.

About TMI

TMI is a leading global consulting and training organization with a focus on implementation. Founded in 1976 in Denmark, it introduced the Time Manager concept—a unique new philosophy—as well as the Time Manager planning tool. Since those early days, TMI has developed a distinctive transformation capability, helping individuals, teams, and organizations.

Today, TMI's focus is on achieving tangible business results for clients in the areas of customer service, leadership, branded culture, personal quality, and performance improvement. The company now has a global footprint in over fifty countries spanning thirty-six languages.

Since its founding, TMI has directly influenced and inspired more than eight million people worldwide. Its focus on engaging and inspiring individuals around a common purpose to give their best is unparalleled. So is TMI's ability to implement and integrate solutions throughout organizations to make them work and make them last—combining short-term results with long-term value. TMI continues to have a positive impact on the lives and performance of hundreds of thousands of individuals working in a wide range of organizations each year.

To a person, TMI consultants are passionate about making a difference! The stories in this book are just a sample of the type of work TMI performs.

For more information and links to our national websites, please visit TMI World at www.TMIWorld.com.